DESIGN BY
DANIA MARTINEZ DAVEY

ROOM RENDERINGS BY
JULIAN LaTROBE

NINA CAMPBELL
&
CAROLINE SEEBOHM

A PANACHE PRESS BOOK
CLARKSON POTTER/
PUBLISHERS

Elsie de Wolfe

A
DECORATIVE
LIFE

Published by Panache Press, an imprint of Clarkson N. Potter, Inc., 201 East 50th Street, New York, New York 10022. Member of the Crown Publishing Group.

CLARKSON N. POTTER, POTTER, PANACHE PRESS, and colophon are trademarks of Clarkson N. Potter, Inc.

Manufactured in Japan

Library of Congress Cataloging-in-Publication Data

Campbell, Nina.
  A decorative life: Elsie de Wolfe/Nina Campbell & Caroline Seebohm.—1st ed.

  1. De Wolfe, Elsie, 1865–1950. 2. Interior decorators—United States—Biography. I. Seebohm, Caroline. II. Title.
NK2004.3.D45C35 1992   747.213—dc20   91-37282   [B]   CIP

ISBN 0-517-58467-0   10 9 8 7 6 5 4 3 2 1   First Edition

CONTENTS

The name Elsie de Wolfe conjures up images of chintz and chinoiserie, leopard skin and shimmering mirrors, green-and-white stripes, glittering international galas, creamy pearls and little white gloves. She was the Queen of Style, the Mother of Invention, and she wove her long and spectacular life (1865–1950) into the stuff of legend.

It did not come easy. Turning her back on an unromantic upbringing, she transformed herself into an actress who could not act but whom everyone wanted to see (her French couture clothes were what counted), an interior decorator before anyone had thought of the term, and a social powerhouse whose scope reached from show business to royalty without drawing a line.

Elsie never drew lines. She stood on her head when she was seventy years old. She was dieting long before anybody knew what a calorie was. She conducted a thoroughly unconventional relationship with theatrical agent Elisabeth Marbury for forty years and, even more scandalously, married at sixty a British diplomat, Sir Charles Mendl—who volunteered subsequently, with great good cheer, "For all I know, the old girl is still a virgin."

Actually, she would have said she had only one love in her life—beauty—and in its pursuit she was indomitable. Even at the end, when she had succeeded beyond her wildest dreams, she never abandoned her quest for the perfect chair, the perfect fabric, the perfect party. If by then it was her parties that hit the headlines, she regarded that as her due. She loved the glitter and the glory and the glamour that her money and her influence could buy.

Frivolous? Perhaps, but with character that could surprise and astonish—as witness the First World War, when she behaved with the utmost courage and dedication. Loving France, she served as a frontline nurse for her adopted country and was awarded both the Croix de Guerre and the Legion of Honor. Indeed, the whole of Elsie de Wolfe's life was like that—a mixture of bravery and ruthlessness, generosity and meanness, substance and superficiality. Her story combines these conflicting elements in a delicious compote, one of whose richness she would most likely have heartily disapproved.

On one of her needlepoint cushions (another Elsie innovation) was embroidered "Who rides a tiger can never descend." That derring-do company surely includes Elsie de Wolfe—a true original with the single-minded determination to achieve her dream, never giving up, whatever the cost. Elsie is doubtless somewhere still riding her tiger, clutching her favorite poodle, all the while making furious suggestions about the redecoration of paradise.

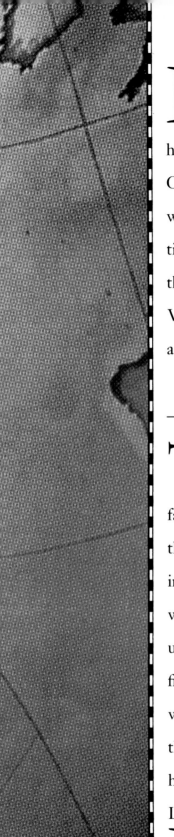

ELSIE

There is hardly a room in America or Europe that has not been influenced by the innovative ideas of Elsie de Wolfe. Chintz, mirrors, trellis, painted furniture, decoupage, black-and-white color schemes—all these decorating techniques and a multitude of others used by designers today come from the armory of this woman warrior, who in 1907 decided to stamp out the stuffy Victorian standards of interior design, and in so doing opened up a new landscape of decoration that endures to this day.

She encompassed her decorating philosophy in three words —*Simplicity*, *Suitability*, and *Proportion*—notions that turned the

THE

design world upside down in the early 1900s, and whose power has never faded. Take, for instance, chintz, the charming printed cotton that graces country houses everywhere. Elsie had seen chintz used in the English houses she visited in the 1880s, and those memories were put to good use when she started decorating herself. She used it in her own house, and all through the Colony Club—her first major commission—to the horror of the membership. But when she assured them that in England one had chintzes in even the grandest rooms, her critics were silenced. Friends, amused at her persistent penchant for the fabric, dubbed her the "Chintz Lady." The title pleased her. "At first people objected to my

PIONEER

bringing chintz into their houses because they had an idea it was poor and mean, and a rather doubtful expedient. On the contrary," she once made abundantly clear, "I feel that it is infinitely better to use good chintzes than inferior silks and damasks."

She particularly liked chintz in bedrooms. "It seems to me there are no more charming stuffs for bedroom hangings than these simple fabrics, with their enchantingly fanciful designs." Not only did she use other people's chintzes, but she designed her own with such success that some, like her famous fern chintz, are still in demand today.

She thought painted furniture went well with chintz. There was a favorite room that she decorated in warm tones of cream, gray, yellow, and cornflower blue—with chintz in a cornflower design that repeated all these colors. She painted the furniture a very soft gray, and then festooned each piece with garlands of cornflowers in soft blues and gray-greens.

She also saw the possibilities of chintz serving as

PRECEDING: *DRIAN'S MURAL OF ELSIE LEAPING THE ATLANTIC.* ABOVE: *THE SALON IN ELSIE'S VERSAILLES HOUSE.* RIGHT: *VERSAILLES BATHROOM.*

2

slipcovers, so that one could make changes "as Marie Antoinette used to do at the Petit Trianon." This charming and practical idea has, of course, been adopted by every decorator in the business, but it was Elsie who first envisioned that "by the use of two sets of covers, one's room may always be clean and inviting, and their color will give glory to the darkest day."

With chintz, Elsie was not only providing color and practicality, but she was also sweeping away the old Victorian notion of heavy plush fabrics, grim colors, and the dark brown paneling that so often accompanied them. She loved a subtle, pale palette—old rose, gray, ivory, or pale blue, with enough white to bring out the light in a room. Her first reaction on seeing the Parthenon was "Beige! Just my color!" Later her favorite color scheme was black and white, and in her

Hollywood heyday she often opted for the bravura boldness of black, white, and dark green —all revolutionary ideas at the time she began to use them.

"Color should be treated kindly, but it should never be allowed to get the best of a house or room," she declared. "And it must be taught to respect the feelings of those who must live with it. Red, for instance, with its great vitality, may very well be too stimulating for one afflicted with too much energy. On the other hand, it may act as an elixir to the shy or the languid. Blue, which is always tractable, is nevertheless somewhat cool by nature and needs a vivid touch to make it genial, especially in a room in which the sun seems conspicuous by its absence."

Cora Potter's apartment decorated by Elsie. Painting by Julian LaTrobe.

Decorator Keith Irvine tells a story that illustrates Elsie's acute sense of color. "She would make an appointment at the client's apartment. Everyone (painters, carpet people, wallpaper hangers, curtain makers) was required to attend. The client would arrive in a big limo. Elsie de Wolfe would then arrive in a bigger one. She would sweep in, survey the room, close her eyes, open them, and then say, 'I see a Queen Anne cabinet over there. I see

6

walls glazed the color of a cooking apple'—and continue in this vein until every piece of furniture, fabric, and color was decided. The only other sound in the room during this monologue was the scratch of pencils as the assembled assistants and artisans wrote on their pads every immortal word of Elsie's marching orders. After that meeting, Elsie would not appear at the site until the actual installation date. Then, looking round, foot tapping and hand on hip, she would demand, 'Why isn't there an apricot silk pillow in that chair?' "

Elsie thought of color not only for the room itself but also for the room's function. For instance, she was always mindful of the problems in using color in a music room or drawing room. "Remember that not only must the room be beautiful in its broad spaces and long lines and soft colors, but it must be a background for the gala gowns of women."

Color infused every aspect of her life. The pioneer who first dyed her hair blue sometimes went one step further and dyed it to match her jewels. At a Halloween party in California, she rejected the seasonal shades suggested for the table centerpieces, which she described as "the brash colors of pumpkins and dead leaves," and instead created the lovely-sounding combination of green apples with silver leaves and white candles. And screened from public sight in a secluded corner of her Beverly Hills garden, her clothesline was strung from posts painted like the boat posts in Venice, with white-and-green stripes.

To bring out the colors in a room, Elsie turned her attention to lighting, in those days a matter of heavily fringed lamps and the dim hangovers of gaslight. Grappling with the problem, still one of the most elusive aspects of interior decoration, Elsie was as autocratic as ever. She hated dark rooms and loathed the ubiquitous Victorian torchères. "Bead covers, fringes, and silk shades all obscure

the light and re-absorb it." She liked the designs of fine old French or Italian lighting fixtures, which were handsome in themselves. "How can one see beauty in a lurid bowl and shade of red glass?"

She used candle-shaped sconces and insisted on candlelight or its electrified approximation, wax candles in her view giving the most beautiful light of all. She invented clip-on shades—precisely the ones used so frequently today—that made light soft and diffuse and more flattering. In the famous Paris bathroom at her avenue d'Iéna apartment, the lights were made of mother-of-pearl in the shape of oyster shells. She annexed natural light with great inventiveness, softening it with translucent curtaining. She loved muslin curtains but detested lace ones, which, "even if they cost a king's ransom, are in questionable taste." She even tackled the problem of outdoor lighting, arranging subtle spotlights in her gardens for her wonderful evening parties, which enhanced the romantic night landscapes.

The only room exempt from her interior-lighting rules was the bedroom, where, she said, "You might as well see yourself for better or for worse." She was entirely practical on the subject. "I think every woman would like to dress always by a blaze of electric light. . . . It is a great thing to know the worst before one goes out, so that even the terrors of the arc lights before our theaters will be powerless to dismay."

Her belief in the importance of lighting oneself included, of course, the requirement of effective mirrors. "Have your mirrors arranged that you get a good strong light by day, and have plenty of lights all around the dressing mirrors for night use. It is a comfort to be on friendly terms with your own back hair!"

Elsie was not only keen on mirrors in the dressing room, she was mirror-mad. She mirrored fireplaces and hung pictures on them. She mirrored cornices. She mirrored walls. She mirrored ceilings. She mirrored sliding panels. She put frames around mirrors like paintings. She cut up mirrors in squares. She mirrored garden walls. She lined any blank space she could find with mirrors, in order to give light, the effect of space, and the feeling of luxury.

Her New York brownstone on East Fifty-fifth Street became known as the "Little House of Many Mirrors" because, as she said, "so much of its charm is the effect of skillfully managed reflections." It was a very narrow house, with dark areas that she deeply disliked. "The secret of its renaissance," she declared, "is plenty of windows and light, color, and mirrors—mirrors—mirrors!"

Elsie's passion for mirrors reflected another of her fascinations, learned in France—"tricking" space to make it larger, lighter, more interesting. Trompe

Left: Anne Morgan's mirrored Manhattan dressing room, in a room rendering by Julian LaTrobe.

l'oeil—the art of deceiving the eye into seeing flat-painted objects as three-dimensional—was a favorite conceit of Elsie's when a

space did not please her. De-coupage was another technique she borrowed from the French. The idea of cutting out pictures from magazines and sticking them on pieces of furniture was positively surreal to most of her contemporaries, but that did not daunt adventuresome Elsie. Her own favorite piece was a desk that she and her secretary, Westy, covered with appliquéd flower prints.

Elsie was an early cham-pion of fine French furniture, the linchpin of her passion for eighteenth-century France. Her respect for FFF was not, needless to say, absolute. If she didn't like the look of a piece, she covered it in chintz or toile or leopard-print velvet. For Elsie was nothing if not eclec-

LEFT: TROMPE L'OEIL ON THE TERRACE AT VERSAILLES. tic. She was per-fectly happy to mix

styles and periods, as long as they worked together. She was also deeply concerned about the cost of things, and while enjoying the patronage of some of the richest people in the country, she never

forgot the word *economy*. In particular, she warned against the purchase of less-than-world-class antiques. "Why lend yourself to possible deception?" she demanded. "If your object is to furnish your home suitably, what need have you of

antiques?" She urged people to respect good reproductions, which she thought "more valuable than feeble originals." She pointed out that a few good wicker chairs would be less expensive and more decorative than "the heavy, stuffy chairs usually chosen by inexperienced people." She liked oak, seeing it with printed linens and books, copper and pewter and gay china. To her, mahogany was the elegantly perfect foil for brocade and fragile china and carved chairs. She insisted on writing tables in as many rooms as possible, for their practicality and their beauty.

Elsie certainly paid as much attention to the arrangement of furniture as she did to the furniture itself. She believed in the wisdom of keeping space intimate, so that there could be multiple conversation centers in a large room, with the seating set up in groups. "No one chair should be too isolated," said Elsie. "Some bashful person who doesn't talk well anyway is sure to take the most remote chair and make herself miserable."

France was also the inspiration for another Elsie "first." She had read about treillage, the artful use of wood-strip trellis, in *La Maison de Plaisance* by Jacques François Blondel, published in 1738. Elsie's brilliant idea was that trellis, origi-

nally used outdoors in gardens, could be very successfully taken indoors. In 1905 she installed it in the garden room of the Colony Club, New York's first club for women. It caused a sensation. After that, she used it frequently to enhance dull spaces and create a garden feeling in the house.

Elsie's interest in gardens was largely decorative. She saw the garden as architectural space, another place where she might make beauty. When she described the garden at her Versailles house, the Villa Trianon, she stressed the colors: "We have tomatoes, the small bright red ones and the yellow ones. . . . Running in a long line between the beds are paved lanes bordered with blue and white flowers." Or, "Everywhere there are blue, white, and rose-colored flowers, planted in great masses against the black-green evergreens."

In spite of these vivid descriptions, Elsie liked flowers mainly for interior use. "Any home must be cold without them." But since her passion was for green and white (outdoors and in), she favored topiary, ivies, and box, arranged beautifully on the green carpet lawn she always called her *tapis vert*. And even dictatorial Elsie recognized the limitations of garden design: "You can select furnishings for a room with fair success, because you can see and feel textures, and colors, and the lines of the furniture and curtains. But gardens are different —you cannot make grass and flowers grow just so on short notice!"

Making grass grow on demand was just the kind of notion Elsie might have chosen to be needlepointed on the decorative cushions that were her invention. "Never complain, never explain," declared one. "A fool and his money are soon invited everywhere," observed another. Perhaps the most expressive of her in-

Left: View of the Versailles garden, as painted by Julian LaTrobe. domitable character is the one that read "Failure only begins when you give up trying to succeed." Elsie never gave up trying.

TREILLAGE

A LA ELSIE

LEFT: Indoor trellis in the de Wolfe tradition—Elsie's pavillion of music, set in the green gardens of the Villa Trianon in Versailles.

OVERLEAF, LEFT: A set of architectural drawings and description for a trellised sun parlor, commissioned by one of Elsie's early clients.

CONTEMPORARY ECHOES OF ELSIE

OVERLEAF, RIGHT: Country sitting room by Denning and Fourcade that is a bower of flowers—full-bloom wallpaper in rosy pinks and reds overlaid with classic wood-strip trellis painted in soft green.

AN ARTISTIC, BUT NOT EXPENSIVE SUN PARLOR

THE UPPER SKETCH SHOWS THE WEST ELEVATION, WHICH IS DIVIDED INTO THREE SECTIONS. THE TWO OUTER SECTIONS HAVE THE LATTICE WORK AND STONE BENCHES. THE CENTER SHOWS A DOUBLE PLATE-GLASS SECTION, FINISHED WITH A LATTICE TOP.

THE SKETCH BELOW THIS GIVES THE DETAILS OF THE EAST ELEVATION, SHOWING THE THREE DOUBLE SECTIONS OF PLATE-GLASS WITH THE LATTICE WORK AT THE TOP.

THE SOUTH ELEVATION HAS THE MARBLE FOUNDATION AND BASIN, SURROUNDED WITH LATTICE WORK, MIRRORED PANELS AT TOP. THE FIREPLACE, COMBINED WITH THE LATTICE WORK, IS SHOWN IN THE NORTH ELEVATION.

ELSIE

ON

STAGE

Elsie de Wolfe should probably never have been a child. Born in 1865, a time when children were meant to be seen and not heard, she was from the beginning a small, opinionated grown-up, waiting till she could abandon her baby clothes and her parents and run her own life. One of her earliest memories was of arriving home from school to find that the de Wolfe drawing room had been redecorated in such dire taste that she promptly threw herself on the floor in a fit of rage. When her father managed to pick her up and ask what was the matter, she shrieked, "It's so ugly! It's so ugly!"

Having tantrums over a choice of wallpaper is not likely to inspire enthusiasm in one's parents. Elsie's father was an attractive but irresponsible doctor with a practice in New York City, and her mother a lawyer's daughter of Scottish descent. Thanks to Dr. de Wolfe's risky financial ventures—which greatly irked his thrifty Scots wife—they lived an unsettled life, moving constantly from one brownstone to another, hovering on the fringes of the Old New York society chronicled by Elsie's contemporary, Edith Wharton.

The de Wolfes kept up appearances, but found their precocious only daughter a less than ideal offspring to ease their social passage among the New York gratin. Elsie continued to lose herself in fantasies of beauty, an escapism that increased in intensity as she grew older. "When other people dream about love or music," she said much later, "I dream about beautiful objects, about pictures and houses. Even when I was a young girl I did that." She determined to make herself beautiful, at least on the inside, by embarking on the most stringent diet and exercise program, anticipating with remarkable perceptiveness what is now a normal health regimen. In retrospect there is something pathetic about this schoolgirl passion, for Elsie was plain, sallow, and lacking in childish charm, a fact her parents were not slow to point out to her. When little Elsie broke a tooth at play, her elegant, handsome father kindly told her she had ruined her one decent feature, which may be why very few photographs exist of Elsie smiling.

In spite of endless money troubles, the de Wolfes managed to send their daughter to Mrs. Macauley's, the proper and preferred school for young ladies on Fortieth Street and Madison Avenue. Here again, however, Elsie endured social ridicule. To save money, her mother dressed her in totally unsuitable clothes, serviceable homemades that the sensitive child must have worn in agony. At fourteen, no doubt with financial economies again in mind, Elsie was sent to Scotland to stay with her mother's cousin, the wife of Dr. Archibald Charteris, one of Queen Victoria's chaplains. Grand though this seemed, Edinburgh was yet another aesthetic nightmare.

PRECEDING: *THEATER PORTRAITS OF ELSIE THE ACTRESS, 1890–1902.* OPPOSITE: *ELSIE ANDERSON DE WOLFE IN THE ARMS OF HER MOTHER, GEORGIANA, 1865.* BELOW: *ELSIE AT FOUR YEARS OLD, AND AT TEN.*

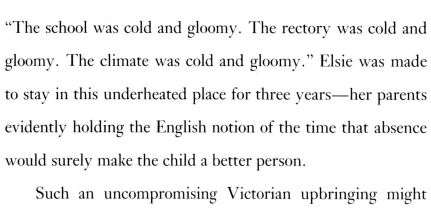

"The school was cold and gloomy. The rectory was cold and gloomy. The climate was cold and gloomy." Elsie was made to stay in this underheated place for three years—her parents evidently holding the English notion of the time that absence would surely make the child a better person.

Such an uncompromising Victorian upbringing might have demolished a lesser mortal. For Elsie, it seems to have been precisely the trial by fire on which she thrived. Thanks probably to the Charteris family's royal connection, in the spring of 1885 this sharp-nosed, thin-lipped, black-eyed young American was presented at court to the Queen herself. The events leading up to this great moment, which encompassed the London social "season," were a revelation to Elsie. For the first time she was exposed to top-quality fashion, chic, and taste, and to the accompanying powerful society, including even the Prince of Wales and his entourage. Wearing her white satin presentation gown made by a London court couturier, with a regulation-length train and a tulle veil with three little white ostrich plumes, Elsie made a solemn vow. "If I am ugly, and I am," she remembered saying to herself, "I am going to make everything around me beautiful. That will be my life. I could steal for beauty. I could kill for it."

Her exposure to the London season, and to the people she met then, marked her irrevocably, giving her her first taste of the world that would ultimately allow her to fulfill her fierce promise to herself without compromise. She later said that as a child she was always delegated the hated chicken legs at the dinner table. "I made myself like it," she said. "The dark meat. But that's the only thing I compromised on."

The life she yearned for really began for Elsie in England. Unlike most debutantes for whom the London season was fertile ground for suitable marriages, it was clear that Elsie would not be ending the year with an engagement ring. She seems to have been mostly disinclined to take part in the hunt, having the good sense to use her interest in fashion and her nose for good contacts to propel her in less romantic but equally fruitful directions. She became the protégée of one of London's American beauties, Cora Potter, an ambitious character of the kind so well observed by Henry James—rich, good-looking, and determined to climb the social ladder. Mrs. Potter had a penchant for amateur theatricals, her own performances attracting the interest of the ever-alert Prince of Wales, thus securing her place in London society. It was with Mrs. Potter that Elsie was able to visit many of England's major country houses, whose spectacular interior decoration, needless to say, she filed away somewhere in her rapacious mind. But it was Mrs. Potter's other passion—the stage—that catapulted Elsie into the first phase of her quest for a place in the beau monde. In 1886, Elsie traveled back to New York with her glamorous friend and promptly embarked on a career in the theater.

ABOVE LEFT: *ELSIE IN HER COMING-OUT DRESS, 1885.* BELOW LEFT: *DEBUTANTE ELSIE IN A PRE-RAPHAELITE POSE.* ABOVE: *ELSIE AND CORA POTTER.*

Elsie the Broadway star.

Initially, Elsie's stage career was on an amateur basis, one of the recognized methods by which a young woman might become accepted in New York society, at that time even more rigid than London's. Although her acting talent was not overwhelming, her energy and adaptability caught the eye of theatrical producer Charles Frohman; and when Elsie's father died, leaving the de Wolfe family practically penniless, Frohman came to the rescue and offered Elsie the then princely sum of two hundred dollars a week to join his acting company.

It was one of Elsie's many lucky breaks. Although in turning professional she was cutting herself off from any hope of a position among society's famous Four Hundred, she was, in typical fearless fashion, facing one of the realities of life she was never to underestimate—the pressing, relentless need for money. "I was a very poor girl," she once said. "I am a self-made woman, and everything you see here I have bought with my own money, but somehow there is never enough. I never, never have enough money to buy all the beautiful things that I want in this world, and to do all the things I want to do."

Charles Frohman's contract also started Elsie off on another crucial path— her lifelong love affair with France. Frohman sent her to Paris in 1890 to study a new play, *Thermidor*, by Victorien Sardou, the celebrated French playwright. Frohman wanted her to star in his production when he brought it to America. This required Elsie—whose accent remained defiantly New York all her life ("poils," "foiniture," "soivants")—to learn French, which she soon spoke with her inimitable accent, but perfectly fluently. While becoming fast friends with Sardou ("We began chatting gaily, he asking and I answering his volley of questions"), Elsie lost no time in recognizing the part of Paris that counted—the haute couture. Worth, Paquin, Redfern, Doucet, Poiret, Molyneux—these were the names dominating European fashion, and theirs were the fashion houses Elsie visited, ordering, studying, honing an eye that would later dazzle New York.

When she returned, she was ready to assume her part in *Thermidor*. It was an unmitigated disaster. "Miss de Wolfe's treatment of the role has nothing to commend it but a sort of mute pathos, which is very well as far as it goes," said the *New York Times*. Mute pathos! How delightful it must have been to read those words later! Elsie, never mute and never pathetic, wasted not a minute with these churlish criticisms. If she wasn't going to be Sarah Bernhardt, she would still get the audiences to come and see her. And indeed they did, particularly the women. They began flocking to her shows—but not for her theatrical interpretations, which she might herself have readily admitted were less than earthshaking. What her followers wanted to see was what she was *wearing*.

Elsie became, in short, star performer—not of the various plays in which she so bravely appeared, but of her own fashion show, modeling in effect the newest, most exciting clothes from the great couture houses of Paris.

Journalists, eager to be first in reporting Elsie's judgments on the French collections, would wait at the dock each time she returned from her annual trips to France. The first Saturday of any Elsie de Wolfe play became known as the "dressmakers' matinee." She would make her entrance in some new confection from Worth or Poiret, and the professional seamstresses in the audience would instantly bring out their pencils, drawing pad at the ready, to produce sketches for their clientele. Forget the performance. Elsie's reviews appeared not in the theater section but on the fashion pages. Overheard dialogue between first-nighters was tellingly reported by one of *Town Topics'* critics: "What did you think of Miss de Wolfe?" asks Maud. Maud's friend answers, "I thought she was splendid in the second dress."

Elsie had once again turned disadvantage into triumph. Not only that, but while an actress she also embarked on one of the most important associations in her life, a friendship that was to take her to her ultimate career destination: from the stage of the theater to the stage of people's living rooms.

In the summer of 1887, when Elsie was still an amateur ingenue, she had appeared in a play sponsored by Cora Potter at the newly opened country club built by tobacco magnate Pierre Lorillard in Tuxedo Park, an enclave of grand houses forty-five miles north of New York City. One of the very exclusive audience that night was Elisabeth Marbury, a thirty-year-old New Yorker of the highest social standing. An unmarried eccentric with scholarly and literary tastes, Miss Marbury lived with her parents on Irving Place. Bessie, as she was called, was not immediately impressed by the looks of Miss de Wolfe—"A lanky, black-eyed, black-haired little creature," she described her disparagingly. However, the "little creature" was not to be disparaged, whatever the circumstance.

Shortly after that summer, Elsie and Bessie were formally introduced at a lunch party given by the distinguished Hewitt sisters (granddaughters of Peter Cooper and later founders of the Cooper-Hewitt Museum). The lunch was to honor the poet Caroline Duer, and Elsie was to read some of Miss Duer's work, which tended to the extreme in the expression of feminine yearnings. Elsie delivered the poems with a feeling that even the most loveless spirit might have found affecting. " 'Sleep, wayward heart,' " read Elsie, her black eyes doubtless flashing madly. " 'If love were sinful, dear/Knowing its price, would we not pay the whole/And count the winning of a life's love here/The wild reality of hearts brought near/Well worth the losing of a phantom soul?' "

The emotional wallop of these lines and their youthful, passionate reader left Miss Marbury reeling. Immediately the two women began seeing each other, mostly on holiday, eventually consolidating a relationship that was to depend more and more on shared interests in the theater and, most important, in France. Bessie's own career was not yet set when she met Elsie; the older woman had dabbled in various enterprises, including poultry breeding and playwriting. When Elsie took the plunge and turned to acting for money, her promoter, Charles Frohman, urged Bessie to become a theatrical agent. Thus both women entered the

ABOVE: *BOUQUETS FOR STYLE, BRICKBATS FOR PERFORMANCE. ELSIE, THE ELEGANT LEADING LADY, IN ONE OF THE FEMME DU MONDE COSTUMES THAT ESTABLISHED HER REPUTATION AS THE MOST CELEBRATED CLOTHESHORSE ON THE BROADWAY STAGE IN THE LAST DECADE OF THE NINETEENTH CENTURY—BUT SHE WON NO APPLAUSE FOR ACTING.*

ranks of Broadway professionals at the same time.

Bessie was a plain, masculine-looking, heavy-voiced, ungainly figure—"Dear, kindly, voluminous Bessie Marbury," P. G. Wodehouse once called her—who had rejected the offer of being presented at court in England in favor of encounters with English intellectuals on the order of Charles Darwin and Thomas Huxley. She admired Elsie's fashion style, sense of fun, and physical fragility. Elsie admired Bessie's high birth, intelligence, interesting circle of friends (mostly single women), and last, but assuredly not least, her money. Elsie had always been attracted to strong, older women, who presumably took the place of a feckless father and a cold mother. And while many observers credited Bessie's sponsorship for Elsie's eventual success and standing, the equation was probably balanced. Elsie's effervescent personality and highly tuned aesthetic sense gave great joy to Bessie, and allowed her to indulge in her long-nurtured dream of a shared life and future.

"Together we sorrowed. Together we rejoiced. Together we failed. Together we succeeded" was Bessie's dedication to Elsie in her 1923 autobiography. This sense of challenging the world together,

ELSIE AND ELISABETH MARBURY AT HOME IN IRVING PLACE.

as intentionally unmarried women who had to work to survive (no easy task at the turn of the century), was the strongest bond in their forty-year shared life.

Later, when on Elsie's side the relationship soured, Bessie remained faithful, even after Elsie, without any warning, married Sir Charles Mendl in 1926. Devastated as Bessie surely was by the defection, she never wavered for an instant in her stalwart support and loyalty to her lifetime love. When Bessie died in 1933, she left all her money and the contents of her Sutton Place house to her adored Elsie. That this was the last gesture of affection from one of the most important people in her life apparently meant nothing to Elsie. In a signal show of unsentimentality she kept no mementos, but instantly sold the lot. It was a sad epilogue, and a powerful demonstration of Elsie's character. Perhaps stemming from her loveless childhood, her capacity for caring as an adult centered on the abstract notion of beauty and beautiful objects rather than any real human equation. Intelligent, gifted, and fiercely partisan when it came to the talents of others, she seemed emotionally unable to make the leap of faith that loving demands—even in the case of someone as totally devoted as Bessie.

For the moment, however, it was honeymoon time for Elsie and Bessie, and the pressing problem was to settle on somewhere to live. In 1892, they found the answer on the southwest corner of Seventeenth Street and Irving Place, a shabby little house in which Washington Irving had once lived. The move was a pivotal step in Elsie's professional life, for it was in this house that she first tried her hand at interior decoration. As she later wrote in rose-colored prose, "It was there that Elisabeth Marbury and I made our first home together. It was there we launched our separate barques on the turbulent sea of new careers for women and saw them come sailing back to us, veritable caravels of good things."

STRIPES

CONTEMPORARY ECHOES OF ELSIE

OVERLEAF, CLOCKWISE FROM LEFT: Gleaming medley of glowing stripes—painted walls, gilt-framed firescreen, and a stripe-turbaned blackamoor—in a burnished living room by Stephen Sills.

Heathea Nye bow-ties curtains of silk taffeta in watercolor stripings of pink, green, and golden yellow to the rings of a twisted gilt pole.

Steamship Moderne settee, designed by Charles Pfister, combines pale satinwood with upholstery striped in aubergine and ivory.

Sol LeWitt's sweep of marble striping on the floor of an apartment in Milan underscores the timeless style of modern Italian design.

SECOND OVERLEAF, CLOCKWISE FROM TOP LEFT: Tie-on slipcovers in thick and thin cotton stripes on the chairs in a dining room designed by Mark Hampton set the character of informal elegance.

The broad stripes of an upholstered bed balance the bold abstract pattern on side chairs in a bedroom designed by Stone and Hutton.

Power play of vivid blue and stark black stripes against red lacquer—on a Paul Poiret chair in Karl Lagerfeld's French country house.

ELSIE

When Elsie and Bessie moved into the Irving Place house, middle-class taste had reached the apogee of decadent Victorianism. Interiors were gloomy with the guilt of double-standard morality, cluttered with the fruits of materialism, swathed in heavy velvets and damasks to mask sins of repression and hypocrisy. The house on Irving Place reflected the times—the thick fringes, dark corners, Turkish rugs, fronded palms, and feeling of airlessness that pervaded the rooms were hallmarks of the period.

It would be inaccurate to suggest that Elsie immediately changed all this. Her summer holidays in France had exposed her to the grandest interiors in

THE

Europe, in particular the lush, gilded style of eighteenth-century French decoration, which could hardly be called light or simple. Thanks to the significant influences of a new friend, Minna, Dowager Marchioness of Anglesey—who lived just outside Paris in suburban Versailles and ran a salon of distinguished artistic and political figures of the fin de siècle—Elsie was introduced to the idea of collecting antiques and art objects for decorative display rather than scholarly preservation. She was encouraged in this by some of Minna's elegant aficionados, including art historian Pierre de Nolhac and the eccentric aesthete Count Robert de Montesquiou, through whom she developed her eye for

DECORATOR

quality and originality. When she finally began to put all this newly discovered knowledge to work in this first home of her own, rather than create a pastiche of sophisticated French culture, Elsie immediately found her unique voice—a voice that spoke clearly and with confidence.

"That little old house asked me the first important questions at the beginning of my career as a decorator," she said later. "And I gave it the answers that made it a happy place." The answers included bringing in light and air, stripping away its Victorian accumulations, heavy paneled walls, somber rugs. "I did the hall in a bright Chinese paper and gray velvet, and I replaced the dirty brown door with one made of small squares of mirrors that doubled the size of the little hall." She used white paint everywhere, French cane chairs, fabrics in soft, warm colors, terra-cotta tiles, transparent lampshades, muslin curtains. It is difficult today to grasp the revolutionary nature of this transformation—as startling as if women's fashions had been transformed from the encumbering crinoline to the liberating miniskirt overnight.

Not surprisingly, there was some talk up and down Fifth Avenue about this new look. The changes, which took place between 1897 and 1898, coincided with the two women's increasing prominence in the New York social scene. By this time, they had been dubbed "the Bachelors" and had an ever-enlarging circle of acquaintances. Bessie in particular, who combined her con-

PRECEDING: *ELSIE THE WOMAN OF BUSINESS.* ABOVE: *THE IRVING PLACE TOWN HOUSE.* RIGHT: *THE IRVING PLACE DINING ROOM—BEFORE AND AFTER ELSIE SWEPT AWAY THE VICTORIAN CLUTTER.*

nection with society's old guard —the Astors, the Hewitts, the Vanderbilts, the Waldorfs— with a sparkling collection of writers and artists acquired through her burgeoning career as a theatrical agent, brought to Irving Place a stimulating mix of people, many of whom clamored to be invited. Edith Wharton, Nellie Melba, Sarah Bernhardt, Oscar Wilde, J. P. Morgan, Ethel Barrymore, and Isabella Stewart Gardner were some of the luminaries at Bessie and Elsie's Sunday teas. In 1901, Henry Adams wrote to a friend, "I went to the Marbury salon and found myself in a mad cyclone of people. Miss Marbury and Miss de Wolfe received me with tender embraces, but I was struck blind by the brilliancy of their world."

THE IRVING PLACE DINING ROOM IN ITS FINAL POLISHED FORM, CIRCA 1910.

While these high-powered visitors may have appreciated the dramatic new interiors designed by Elsie, the idea that decorating could be a career for her could hardly have been further from their minds. Decorating, at that time, was not a profession at all, let alone gainful employment for Miss de Wolfe, who was still doggedly plugging on in the theater. For three more years after Henry Adams's dazzled visit to the Irving Place salon, Elsie continued to visit France—and especially Versailles—with Bessie, and to be cast in plays that provoked less-than-enthusiastic reviews. Although the two women expanded their range as party givers both in France and in New York, Elsie's acting aspirations finally began to flag. When a Pinero play entitled *A Wife Without a Smile*, starring Elsie, closed after just one miserable week in December 1904, she bit the bullet. Over Christmas that year, without a smile, Miss de Wolfe retired from the stage.

She wrote later—with almost endearing dramatization—that the time after her abrupt departure from the theater was the darkest interlude in her life. "The tether with which I had hitched my chariot to the stars had snapped. The debris of my scattered dreams was a sad reality for me to contemplate. I had some terrible moments in which I was overwhelmed by my failure to become a great actress. I could not but feel that the mediocrity of which I have always had a horror was closing in on me."

It is not surprising that even tenacious Elsie—nearly forty, without career, without money, without prospects—was confronting the abyss. But with that combination of good fortune and timing that seems to have marked her life, within a year she had not only leapt over the abyss but was galloping energetically toward a height few other women of her age, time, and class could ever have contemplated.

While Elsie faced an uncertain future, Bessie Marbury was becoming increasingly successful. Sensitive to her friend's plight, Bessie began to focus on talents other than Elsie's dubious acting abilities: her fashion sense; her enthusiasm for the decorative arts, particularly the French; her eye for color and proportion; and her way with rooms. Visitors to the Washington Irving house had sometimes commented on the interiors and expressed a desire to see the same ideas put to use in their own homes. Why shouldn't Elsie dispense her advice for money?

In 1895, an article by Mrs. Candace Wheeler suggesting that interior decoration might provide a profession for women had appeared in *Outlook* magazine. In 1897, the Hewitt sisters launched their museum of decorative arts and design, the Cooper-Hewitt, opening the door to the notion of appreciating and collecting textiles and antiques, and also inspiring contemporary designers. In that same year, Edith Wharton and Ogden Codman published *The Decoration of Houses*, in which they exposed the frailties of contemporary Victorian taste and urged a reconsideration of European standards of simplicity and elegance.

In short, the temper of the times was moving toward a new mood in interior design. When Elsie printed her first business cards—embellished with the small wolf-cum-nosegay crest that would become her trademark—she probably little knew not only how perfectly she was in tune with a small cultural revolution but that she was going to be a player of such enormous influence.

Her first professional break could hardly have been improved upon—the decoration of New York's Colony Club. As a clubhouse, Stanford White had designed a grand brick building on Madison Avenue and Thirtieth Street for those women, resentful of their husbands' elegant retreats, who wanted their own place for use as a social center or base of operations when visiting from out of town. Needless to say, Elsie's connections—not least her own close companion, Bessie Marbury, who was on the founding board of the Colony Club, and Anne Morgan, another new and influential friend —helped her get the commission. There was some resistance, for Elsie was neither an antiques dealer nor an architect, at that time the only recognized house-furnishing professionals. She was also untrained, inexperienced, and a woman to boot. It was Stanford White himself who gave his categorical imprimatur: "Give the job to Elsie," he said, "and let the girl alone. She knows more than any of us."

He was right. Elsie's work at the Colony Club left no doubt that she knew what she was doing. Patterning her choices on her memories of English country houses, she used glazed chintzes, light curtains, tiled floors, wicker furniture, lacquered chairs, painted wall panels, and—most startling of all to the ladies who lunched—treillage. She daringly dressed the room leading off the main drawing room entirely in dark green trellis, with a fountain, lanterns, and trellised cornices and friezes. The overall effect was delightfully reminiscent of an eighteenth-century conservatory. A garden room in the confines of a respectable New York ladies' club? Tongues wagged in absolute astonishment. It was Elsie's first bravura performance on her new stage and it paid off handsomely.

OPPOSITE: *THE TRELLIS ROOM IN THE COLONY CLUB.*
ABOVE: *THE ORIGINAL COLONY CLUB BUILDING ON MADISON AVENUE. BELOW: A COLONY CLUB BEDROOM.*

CHINTZ

A LA ELSIE

LEFT: Julian LaTrobe's rendering of a model de Wolfe bedroom—upholstery and curtains covered in a commanding chintz pattern, with the pale walls painted a soft complementary color.

CONTEMPORARY ECHOES OF ELSIE

OVERLEAF, CLOCKWISE FROM LEFT: Brilliant color and bold scale in a bravura print unifies the eclectic components of a French salon.

Pristine unglazed chintz printed with prim nosegays emphasizes the antic architecture of a bedroom in a Swedish waterside cottage.

Chintz and miniature plaids paired by Zajac and Callahan in the canopy, headboard, and cover of a bed with Louis XVI manners.

A glimpse of wall and bed canopy covered in classic toile de Jouy the color of terra-cotta, in a guestroom of a French country house.

Geoffrey Bennison's flower-bouquet
chintz covers the walls of an English
bed-sitting room. The bed is hung
with the same signature chintz and
separated from the rest of the room
by unpainted antique double doors.

57

VILLA TRIANON

ELSIE

It had taken Elsie two long years to turn out her Colony Club triumph. While expanding her business, coping with dealers, learning the trade, she had also kept one vision firmly in mind—the vision of the small house in Versailles that Bessie had bought for them both in 1905, the Villa Trianon. This was the place on which Elsie would shower her love, her talents, her energies, and her unending loyalty for the next forty-five years. "Without it," she wrote, "the pattern of my life could never have been woven in such bright hues."

IN

Elsie and Bessie had first stumbled upon the property in 1903, when they vacationed in a nearby rented cottage during the waning days of Elsie's inexorably fading theatrical career. The house had been part of the great Versailles palace complex built during the reign of Louis XIV and added on to in the early nineteenth century under the Duc de Nemours, son of King Louis Philippe. Since the 1848 revolution the place had been abandoned—but its crumbling, faded elegance, the interiors and gardens almost totally destroyed after fifty years of neglect, only whetted the appetites of the two Francophile romantics, particularly the one whose ideals were already so firmly planted in the eighteenth century. Elsie saw herself as part of the Versailles court—as indeed did others, among them

LOVE

her friend Pierre de Nolhac, who insisted, "You are not a

modern woman. You are a ghost who has come back to us from the court of Louis XV." This small and rustic cottage, a tottering monument to a bygone golden age, represented to Elsie the fulfillment of a lifetime's passion. It had taken more than a year of haggling with the labyrinthine French bureaucracy—the deeds of the villa gave the King of France right-of-way through the grounds in perpetuity —but finally the two Americans found themselves the owners (in Bessie's name) of a run-down, impractical ruin on the borders of the royal park of Versailles.

Even Elsie's energies might well have been expected, at this point, to have been used up on her decoration of the Colony Club. *Au contraire.* While designing a revolutionary new look for the ladies of metropolitan New York, she had also been drawing on all the memories of romantic rooms and homes she had visited in England and France, crystallizing her plans for the restoration, revival, and triumphant new life of her true *amour*, the Villa Trianon. She never wavered in her devotion to this French paradise, or in her attention to its needs. She never wanted to do anything other than to "lavish on that house all the infinite care that a house wants, that anything in this world you love deserves."

Lavish she did, sometimes to the alarm of the person footing the bills. "When Elisabeth Marbury bought the Villa Trianon at Versailles," Elsie once said

blithely, "I used to sit around by the hour, dreaming of the way it would look when it had been done over. 'Come out of your trance,' my dear Bessie would say. 'When you go into your trances, it is always so expensive for me.' " Whatever Bessie's reservations, Elsie brooked no compromise on the Villa Trianon. Her first demand was the installation of five bathrooms—an instruction that flabbergasted the neighbors, who were convinced that the bath-mad Americans must suffer from some dire skin disease. But Elsie's steely resolve silenced even the harshest critics, and with her confident directions and Bessie's generous checks, the Villa Trianon was transformed into an eighteenth-century dream house. The bachelor pair had spent their summers in France over a number of years and, under the expert tutelage of her worldly neighbors Minna Anglesey and Robert de Montesquiou, Elsie had developed a remarkable eye for the decorative arts and for "old shopping," as antiquing was called by her circle. Haunting the shops of the Paris antiquarians and *fabricants du tissus*, scouring the byways of the countryside for château finds, becoming a familiar figure to private dealers, she assembled a marvelous collection of objects with impeccable provenance to fill the gracefully proportioned rooms. Paneling, silks, screens, paintings, antiques, chandeliers—all combined into a harmonious entity that would have delighted her ghostly patroness, Marie Antoinette.

The Villa Trianon was Elsie's faithful friend and lover, even when all else failed. She would speak of it almost every day of her life. "Whether I think of it in retrospect or wander through its rooms or gardens, I am filled with gratitude for all the things that it has brought me." Over the years, a third companion, Anne Morgan, joined the two women in the house, sharing expenses and contributing to the dazzling entertainments presented there.

Labels visible on the map image: *Vers Suresnes*, *Vers Longresson*, *Ville d'Avray*, *Côte de Saint Cloud*, *NORD*, *B. St Antoine*, *Côte de Picardie*, *Porte de Versailles*, *B. de la Reine*, *Vers le Palais*, *VERSAILLES*, **VILLA TRIANON**

ABOVE: *POSTCARD DIRECTIONS TO THE VILLA TRIANON, FROM A MURAL BY DRIAN.*

Leaving America in May or June each year, tired out with the "breathless business of living," Elsie would find rest and strength in the Villa Trianon, and each year she would be restored by its perfection and its ambience of serenity and grace. "We breakfast on the stone terrace, with boughs of trees and clouds for our roof, and as we look out over the masses of blue flowers and the smooth *tapis vert*, over the arched treillage with its fountains and its marbles, the great trees in back of our domain frame the supremely beautiful towers of the *Château le Magnificent*, and we are far happier than anyone deserves to be in this wicked world."

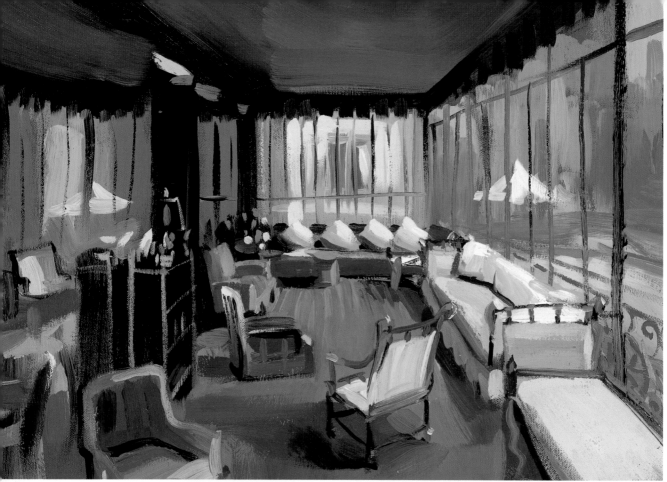

A roster of Villa Trianon rooms. Clockwise from above: Julian LaTrobe's rendering of the terrace sunroom; Elsie's bedroom, as painted by William Rankin; the state guestroom; Elsie's sitting room, by Rankin; the boiserie-paneled salon. Overleaf, clockwise from top left: Rankin's painting of the treillage music pavilion; the library; Elsie's bathroom.

ELSIE

During the years between the Colony Club coup and the First World War, Elsie was well able to keep the wicked world at bay. Her career was taking off. She had begun to buy antiques and paintings in Europe on a grand scale, bringing them back to the United States to resell to her American customers. An inveterate self-promoter, she came up with the idea of renovating a Manhattan town house to display her talents. Elsie's

STRIKES IT

invention—reincarnated today as the decorator's show house— was typically dramatic: take a run-down old brownstone, reconstruct it, decorate it, and demonstrate to the world how avant-garde are your ideas about interior design.

To help with the architectural aspects of the plan, Elsie picked Ogden Codman, who had collaborated with Edith Wharton on *The Decoration of Houses*. Between them, Elsie and Codman presented the epitome of what current fashion required of a perfect town house. In so doing, they also initiated an architectural revolution by ripping out the familiar "stoop"—the flight of

RICH

stairs that led from the street to the second-floor front entry of conventional brownstones. They brought the front door down to ground level, improving the space of these narrow houses to a marked degree.

Her point proved, Elsie sold the demonstration house and proceeded to work her decorating wiles on a new nest, bought with Bessie, at 123 East Fifty-fifth Street. Christened "The Little House of Many Mirrors," this brownstone was done in a much grander style than the Irving Place ménage. Elsie had more and better furniture, her eye was increasingly educated, her taste refined, her budget larger. The house turned out a triumph—and was another trump card in Elsie's name and fame game.

In 1912 Elsie was still the only woman decorator in the United States, and in 1913 she published her first book. *The House in Good Taste* was a collection of how-to articles on interior decoration that had appeared under her name in *The Delineator*, a popular magazine of the time. (They were mostly ghostwritten by Ruby Ross Goodnow, who learned so much from this collaboration that she quit journalism

and, as Ruby Ross Wood, became a successful decorator herself.) Apart from the Wharton-Codman opus, nothing had yet been published on this rapidly expanding business, and with her book Elsie began to reach a wider audience, giving her even more authority in the increasingly competitive field.

But perhaps the most significant event in Elsie's career during the years directly preceding the First World War was her encounter with tycoon Henry

Clay Frick, who, at the height of his power and financial success, hired the tiny female dynamo to decorate the private rooms of his new mansion on Fifth Avenue, which was to house his fabulous art collection and be turned into a museum after his death. Frick offered Elsie a 10 percent commission on everything she bought, provided she took no commissions from dealers.

It was a once-in-a-lifetime opportunity, and Elsie grabbed it with her customary confidence. The story goes that on being presented with her plans, the illustrious millionaire, known to be a man of few words, stared at them for some time and then simply asked to see an alternate presentation. Elsie, who did not have one, thought for a moment and then said, "Mr. Frick, when I draw up a set of plans there is no second choice. There is only what I show you. The best." She was right, of course. For Frick she could finally prove her credo of beauty. She hunted the world for objects that would meet her standard of excellence, and she did not flinch at the cost. She bought from individuals and estates wherever she could find them, and everything she purchased was of the finest quality, including the treasures of Bagatelle, the legendary eighteenth-century château in the Bois de Boulogne—which Frick bought in thirty minutes for an estimated three million dollars. In that half hour Elsie became a rich woman.

Through these heady years, Elsie was also making another important new acquaintance. The youngest daughter of financier J. P. Morgan, Anne Morgan had come across Elsie de Wolfe over the Colony Club commission. She had first visited the Villa Trianon in 1907, and quickly became an intimate of both Bessie's and Elsie's. While Anne tended to dress in masculine fashion like Bessie and, like her friends, was a confirmed bachelor, she differed from them in that she had a powerful, if latent, social conscience.

ABOVE RIGHT: *ONE OF THE TREASURES FROM THE HENRY CLAY FRICK HOUSE.*

70

In the beginning, Anne's efforts at social involvement had been rather arbitrary, but the 1911 Triangle Shirtwaist Company fire in New York, which had shown the world the wretched working conditions for women, had also brought into focus Anne's own feelings about women's suffrage. However, in 1912, when Alva Vanderbilt Belmont led a battle for women's rights in Newport, and later organized a suffrage parade down Fifth Avenue, it was Elsie, and not Anne or Bessie, who joined the march. Anne disliked the political aspects of the movement, and Bessie, in a perversely reactionary mood, declared, seemingly without irony, that real success for women meant "to marry happily and have children and a home."

Perhaps based on her marching experience, perhaps because in 1912 skirts were narrow and difficult to maneuver in, Elsie asked that the hem of a suit she was ordering from a Madison Avenue dressmaker be raised six inches. This innocent request, purely practical in origin, caused a minor scandal when Elsie went on holiday to Paris, where her neat ankles acquired the status of a feminist emblem. By the end of the summer, "le walking suit" was the new fashion.

Elsie's further foray into political radicalism was also of her own making. On

returning to the United States in the fall of that year, she brought with her, as was her custom, a wardrobe of new French clothes, on which a vigilant customs official slapped an import duty of 60 percent. Elsie paid the tariff but immediately decided to take the United States Customs Bureau to court in order to get it back. In so doing, she uncovered the unpleasant fact that she had to pay taxes on her hard-earned income at the same rate as those blessed with income that was unearned. Elsie instantly filed another suit, this time to change what she judged to be an unfair tax law. "I learned that the rate of taxation on my earnings was exactly the same as that on the income of those who had inherited their money. In other words, my profits, which were in reality the only profits I had, were taxed, while the capital of those who sat idly at home cutting coupons was immune."

In the end she lost the tax case but got her import duty back. While the rulings may have seemed half a loaf, the experience gave Elsie some welcome national exposure, spreading her reputation as a feisty female. This diversion from the rarefied atmosphere of Fifth Avenue drawing rooms into the real world was shortly, thanks to the looming tragedy in Europe, to become a major commitment.

ABOVE: *The de Wolfe decorating signature, in a sitting room for Anne Morgan and in Elsie's bedroom. Right: The 55th Street drawing room, in pastel by Walter Gay.*

CHINOISERIE

CONTEMPORARY ECHOES OF ELSIE

LEFT: Lacquer, wallpaper paneling, bird-and-branch printed fabric—chinoiserie signatures in a room designed by Denning and Fourcade.

OVERLEAF, CLOCKWISE FROM TOP LEFT: Mario Buatta chooses the graceful formality of an eighteenth-century Chinese paper for the walls of the Dillon Room at Blair House, the White House guest residence.

A pair of Chinese wall hangings from the 1700s flanks a door leading to the garden of the Villa Windsor set in the Paris Bois de Boulogne.

A Chinese Chippendale mirror finds its natural habitat against the tracery of a period chinoiserie wallpaper in an English drawing room.

ELSIE'S

TRUE

GRIT

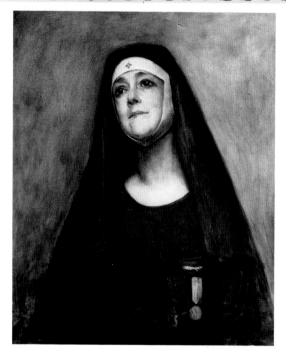

PRECEDING: *ELSIE IN WORLD WAR I. FROM LEFT: FRONTLINE NURSES, ELSIE AND THE BARONNE HENRI DE ROTHSCHILD; INVESTED WITH THE LEGION OF HONOR; SURROUNDED BY ALLIED OFFICIALDOM, COMMANDANT PAUL-LOUIS WEILLER AT LEFT. LEFT: ELSIE THE ANGEL OF MERCY, IN A DECIDEDLY DRAMATIC PORTRAIT BY MARIETTE COTTON.*

By the summer of 1914, Elsie, Bessie, and Anne—the "Versailles triumvirate"—were safely ensconced as usual in their pastoral Parisian suburb. Blissfully ignorant of the ominous rumblings from Germany and the Balkans, Bessie and Anne left in July to take their annual cure at Brides-les-Bains, near the Italian border, while Elsie, in Baden-Baden, was planning a post-spa trip to Spain.

On August 3, Germany declared war on France. Elsie's French chauffeur, having driven her and her maid in her Rolls-Royce as far as Perpignan, agreed to take them across the border to Barcelona before returning, as directed by his government, to report for war. Borders were being closed, and suddenly Elsie found herself stranded, without money, in Spain. Meanwhile, Bessie and Anne were equally left in the lurch in Brides-les-Bains. The three friends finally made contact by telegram and agreed to meet in Biarritz. For Elsie, this meant another attempt at crossing the border. Even though her train did not make it, Elsie herself—in concert with her maid, two Pekingeses, and seven pieces of luggage —did not falter. She completed the journey by horse and cart.

Biarritz was only a temporary respite. It rapidly became clear that war was going to disrupt the trio's lives, particularly when they learned that the Villa Trianon was under German attack. Returning to Paris, Elsie and Anne obtained permission to travel through the military zone of Versailles for a last visit to their beloved home, only to find that the American ambassador, Myron Herrick, had been there before them and had arranged for the house to be placed under American protection. Turning the villa over to the Red Cross to be used as a hospital —doubly guaranteeing its survival—the women went back to Paris. Shattered by the devastation they saw on a tour of the Marne battlefield, the three soon decided to return to the United States to start relief work on behalf of the Allies.

Elsie's formidable energies had found a new and nobler cause than she had thus far encountered—a cause, unfortunately, that was destined to tear apart the most enduring relationship she had ever forged. The issue was clear-cut: Bessie wished to do her war work on American shores; Elsie was eager to return at once to the fray in France. For the first time in their nearly thirty years together, Bessie and Elsie were in direct opposition.

Bessie's undiminished love for her tough-minded friend was never more evident than in this new crisis. For eighteen months, she managed to keep Elsie in New York with the distraction of designing theatrical sets for the musical productions of such talents as P. G. Wodehouse and Cole Porter. And decorating commissions continued to roll in. But Elsie's heart was elsewhere. "I was miserable,"

she wrote later. "For I could not forget the misery I had seen, and my desire to go to France ate into me day and night. I felt as if I were swimming in glue." When Bessie briefly left town in June of 1916, Elsie sent her a telegram announcing she was sailing for Europe with Anne the following day. Bessie rushed back to find her friends packing. Acknowledging defeat, the older woman made preparations to join them on the risky sea voyage, but the inevitable break had begun. They arrived once more at the Villa Trianon together. When Bessie returned to the United States later that summer, however, she traveled alone.

While Anne threw herself into the American Fund for French Wounded, Elsie took up the gauntlet for a controversial new treatment for bomb and gas burns—Ambrine, a hot-wax skin sealant that promoted healing. Haunted by the terrible suffering from burns she had seen on the battlefield, Elsie volunteered to work in the Ambrine Mission outside Paris. For four months she was exposed to some of the worst aspects of war, dressing suppurating wounds, surrounded by screams of pain, dealing with the most basic human needs of the French and

British soldiers—mostly enlisted men, boys in fact—whose bodies were rotting so badly that, like most of the other nurses, she was forced to take up smoking in order to diffuse the smell. Yet this high priestess of beauty not only endured these terrible conditions but transcended them. In what was surely her finest hour, Elsie became an inspiration to her patients, in constant attendance, holding their hands, urging and even bullying them back to health.

In late October, Elsie returned to the United States to raise funds for Ambrine. She was once more a sensation. People who were accustomed to her opinions on mirrors, trellis, and decoupage were suddenly confronted by a new Florence Nightingale, describing experiences that shocked the hardiest observers, showing films that caused people to faint in horror. The fastidious party giver, queen of good taste, arbiter of fashion, was revealing the kind of courage and determination worthy of a stage heroine.

She returned triumphantly to France with seventeen new ambulances equipped to administer the Ambrine treatment and remained with the mission until the end of the war. During her occasional Sunday off, she went back to the

OPPOSITE: *ELSIE'S STAGE SET FOR THE 1915 MUSICAL COMEDY* NOBODY'S HOME. RIGHT: *ELSIE IN NEW YORK, 1915—FUND-RAISING FOR AMBULANCES FOR THE ALLIES.* FAR RIGHT: *ELSIE AT WAR'S END, 1919—MODESTLY CONCEALING HER MEDALS.*

relative peace and comfort of the Villa Trianon. Many of the rooms were now hospital wards, but the house still attracted the world of high-level social, military, and political figures. They flocked there for a little rest and relaxation with the famous Versailles hostess, whose energy and optimism never flagged.

Elsie's last great act of bravery during the war was to help the Ambrine Mission evacuate—first to Compiègne and then to Saint Aumont—in flight from the approaching Germans. Under fire, she kept a diary. "The usual round of dressings during the A.M. I am especially interested in No. 44; poor man, his poor face is all twisted and the fingers of his right hand are grown together. This would not have happened had he been sent to the Ambrine in the beginning. Now it is too late." When the hospital was safely installed at Saint Aumont in the spring of 1918, Elsie returned to Compiègne in the face of the German advance. Westy, Elsie's secretary, later told the story:

> "She refused to leave [Compiègne] until all her wounded were evacuated, and then she didn't go, and did a typical Lady Mendl thing. In the basement of the house in which they spent most of the time, on account of the heavy shelling, she remembered that a few cans of gasoline had been left. She did not want these to fall into the hands of the Germans. Anyone else would have spilled out the gasoline and set it on fire. But Lady Mendl got someone to help her and buried the cans, and she made a sketch of the place and put a broken wheelbarrow there to mark the spot. All this under fire. Finally they put her on one of the last ambulances and made her leave. The tide of battle turned after that and she went back, and they were still there, the cans of gasoline."

The grateful French government awarded Elsie the Croix de Guerre and later the Legion of Honor, but her performance rated much higher than a piece of ribbon. No one could ever again say that Elsie was a shallow, empty-headed social butterfly. She had taken on a terrible duty of her own free will, and had executed it fearlessly, with total commitment and the utmost courage.

BLACK&WHITE

CONTEMPORARY ECHOES OF ELSIE

OVERLEAF: A gleaming baby grand is the sleek centerpiece of the living room in a Manhattan penthouse by interior designer David Salomon.

SECOND OVERLEAF, FROM LEFT: A checkered black-and-white ceramic lamp—dramatic counterpoint to a matte-black bedside table.

White canvas, polished black leather, checkerboard chair back, and the powerful punctuation of cowhide rugs combine in the timbered living room of a house in the deep green woods of northern Maine.

Now since my sweetheart Sal met Miss
    Elsie de Wolfe,

The leading decorator of the nation,

It's left that gal with her mind simply full'f

Ideas on interior decoration. . . .

And so she's put all color from her sight

And everything she owns is black and white.

She's got a black and white dress,
    a black and white hat,

A black and white doggie and
    a black and white cat. . . .

She's got a black and white shack

And a new Cadillac

In a black and white design.

All she thinks black and white

She even drinks Black and White,

That black and white baby of mine.

Lyrics from Cole Porter's "That Black and White Baby of Mine"

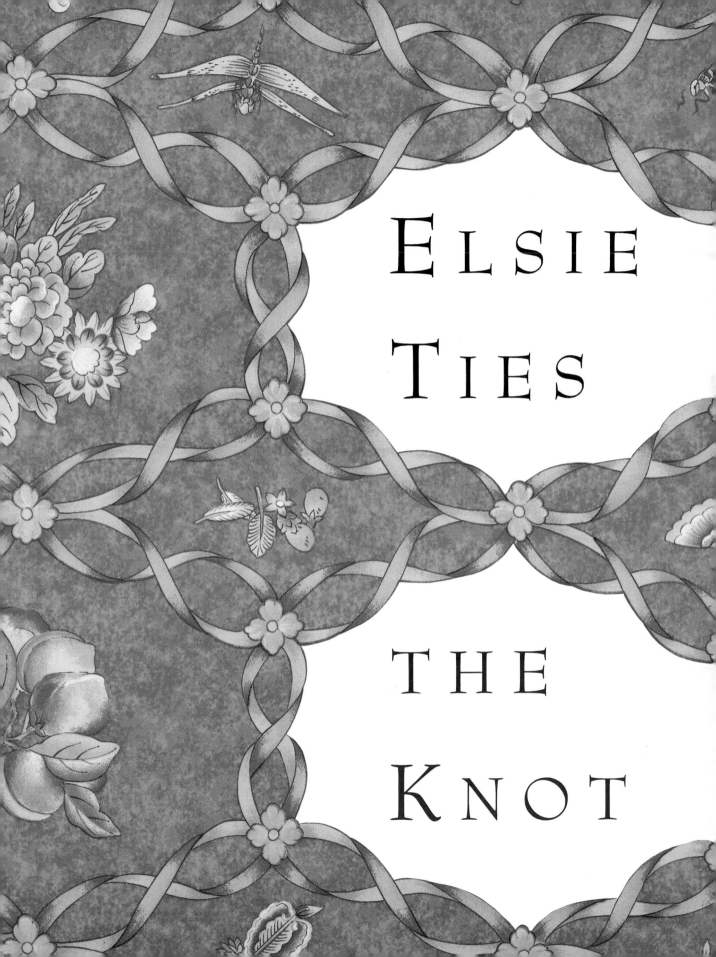

ELSIE

TIES

THE

KNOT

The war was a watershed experience for Elsie. Exposure to the most extreme aspects of human anguish strengthened her determination to make beauty and pleasure the linchpins of her life. In tapping an unexpected source of courage, she also discovered a freedom in living on her own that she had never before known. With that discovery came the realization that her life with Bessie was over. In the

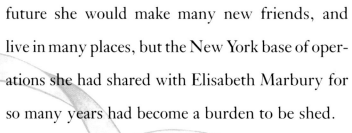

future she would make many new friends, and live in many places, but the New York base of operations she had shared with Elisabeth Marbury for so many years had become a burden to be shed.

The external manifestation of this change was that when the lease expired on the Fifty-fifth Street brownstone in which they had lived together since 1910, Bessie bought a new house on Sutton Place for herself alone. A number of others in the New York social circle of independent women—including Anne Morgan, Mrs. Chauncey Olcott, and Anne Vanderbilt—also bought houses in this off-beat part of town, causing talk of an alleged "Sapphic enclave" that was bruited about in the gossip columns. Elsie, of course, was

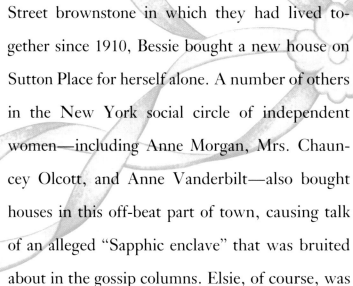

the official decorator and did a small suite as a pied-à-terre for herself at Bessie's. But the two old friends were destined, from now on, to go their separate ways.

And Elsie's way was in the direction of Europe. While Bessie committed herself more and more to life in America, with ever-tighter ties to Broadway, Hollywood, and the Democratic party, and played host to a distinguished circle of friends in Sutton Place, Elsie began collecting a new circle of her own, most of whose members were based in France and Italy. She took up with two bright American bachelors-about-town—Johnnie McMullin, a roving *Vogue* fashion columnist, and Tony Montgomery, a sometime decorator, who lived outside Paris. She also fell into the clutches of Elsa Maxwell, whose parties were legendary. She visited Cole and Linda Porter in France and Venice, Bernard Berenson in Florence, and Gerald and Sara Murphy on the French Riviera, where her decorating style was in great demand. Her trademark trellis, stripes, and mirrors meshed perfectly with the glorious and still "undiscovered" Mediterranean landscape of the lush Côte d'Azur, and her oft-proclaimed maxims of color and comfort matched the holiday mood and style of life in Southern France.

It was during one of the Porters' house parties on the Riviera that Elsie met Sir Charles Mendl for the first time. Mendl, a fifty-five-year-old British embassy functionary, came from an obscure background but demonstrated a charm and joie de vivre that were not in the least obscure, and Elsie decided this was the man she would marry. The question might arise at this point: Why would she want to marry anybody? It was clear that her sexual predilections,

if indeed they had ever been a motivating force, were by now happily sublimated in her pursuit of beauty. In 1926, the year she married Sir Charles, she was in her sixties—older than the husband designate by some half-dozen years— an age that does not encourage flexibility in a relationship as intimate and demanding as marriage.

Elsie's own description of the romance reads reasonably enough. "We moved in the same circles. We spoke the same language. We took a real delight in each other's company. For ten years he was a member of my weekly house parties at the Villa Trianon, and a frequent guest at my tiny

house in Paris. When one has passed the portals of middle life one's greatest necessity is companionship. Charles and I had a deep affection for each other, and mutual respect and admiration. We suddenly made up our minds to be married, naming the tenth of March as our wedding day." The ceremony took place at the British embassy in Paris. The bride wore Chanel, and the witnesses included Anne Vanderbilt and the British and American ambassadors.

The unexpected nuptials astonished all of Elsie's friends. Companionship was surely an important element in her decision to marry. Elsie in her sixties had the energy level of a woman in her thirties, and she needed a constant "fix" of people to entertain her and be entertained by her. A live-in audience and foil must have seemed an attractive proposition. Moreover, in those days, a *femme sole* had social disadvantages of which Elsie was perfectly conscious. If she could not only eradicate those disadvantages but also enhance her social standing with the addition of a title to her name, so much the better. Presumably the same benefits applied from Sir Charles's point of view. He found her fun, and richer than he was—though less rich, it turned out, than he had hoped. There would clearly be no sexual complications, and he would be

allowed to continue pursuing young ladies to his heart's content—his reputation for romantic liaisons was well known—as long as he was discreet. Their social lives intertwined pleasingly enough. He must have found her vivid personality both entertaining and affecting—and sometimes disconcerting—as evidenced by Ludwig Bemelmans's story of his first meeting with Sir Charles. First of all, Sir Charles tripped over a Madame de Pompadour footstool that Elsie had just taken

ABOVE LEFT: *ELSIE AND CHARLES IN THE DUKE OF CONNAUGHT'S GARDEN AT BEAULIEU ON THEIR HONEYMOON.* CENTER LEFT: *CHARLES AT HIS EASE.* BELOW LEFT: *ELSIE AND CHARLES AT ODDS.* ABOVE: *AN ALFRESCO LUNCH PARTY AT VERSAILLES.*

out of storage and placed in the sunlight because it had been "lonesome and cold."

He lay on the floor, very still.

"My God, he's dead," said Lady Mendl.

"Nonsense," answered Sir Charles. "I'm not dead. Having played polo all my life, I simply know how to fall. When one falls one remains absolutely still for a minute. Now don't anyone bother helping me up."

He remained quiet for what seemed a long time.

"Are you resting, dear?" asked Lady Mendl.

"Yes, I'm resting," said Sir Charles.

"Well, don't overdo it."

Sir Charles was watching the dial on his wristwatch. At the end of a minute he got up.

Lady Mendl put one fist to her hip and stamped her foot. "You search the world for beauty," she said, "for beautiful things to live with; you fill your home with the most exquisite pieces and you place them right; all is perfect, and then in comes your husband wearing that awful coat—that inseparable, impermeable, confounded trench coat—and ruins the effect so carefully established."

The end of this story is that Elsie asks her husband to go out of the room and come in again. "I would love to see you come into this house without that coat." Sir Charles obliges.

The marital pattern between the odd couple was soon established. Sir Charles maintained his bachelor digs in Paris (Elsie also at that time bought a tiny pied-à-terre on the rue Laroux), frequently giving his own celebrated soirées, which included a lot of pretty women, some very good claret, and an approximation of lieder. Sir Charles prided himself on his voice, one of the few elements of his personality Elsie could not appreciate, having not a single musical bone in her body. (Bessie and Elsie often used to entertain the great opera singer Nellie Melba during their years in the Irving house, but never asked her to sing. "We love you not because you are a prima donna, but in spite of it!" Elsie told her firmly.) On weekends, Sir Charles would join his wife at the Villa Trianon, where more parties and entertainments would pass the time most agreeably.

Elsie maintained her other intimate friendships. But the person hurt most because of her changed status was Bessie Marbury, who, in an unforgivable oversight, had not been warned about the marriage. Although their lives had become almost entirely separate, Bessie at least felt that her friendship with Elsie was binding for all time, and this betrayal was a deep shock. Charles Mendl himself, promising he was no rival for Elsie's heart, helped soothe Bessie's wrath. In truth, of course, Elsie's heart was with neither Charles nor Bessie. If she had one at all, it was firmly entrenched in the Villa Trianon—shared later with her bathroom in her Paris apartment on the avenue d'Iéna.

BELOW: A SELF-PORTRAIT OF HILDA WEST, ELSIE'S FAITHFUL, LONG-TERM FACTOTUM.

While friends came and went at the Villa Trianon, there was one constant: Hilda West. Her secretary, companion, housekeeper, party planner, and maid-of-all-work, Westy had risen through the ranks of Elsie's Manhattan office, and for the next three decades, she dealt with the everyday and far-into-the-night details of Elsie's whirlwind life, smoothing the path for her peripatetic employer in New York, Paris, and Beverly Hills—along the way winning the respect and affection of everyone in Elsie's world with her spirit, grace, and discretion. Devoted to Elsie's interests, a willing slave to Elsie's tyranny of taste, Westy gave over her own life to that of her impossible, fascinating, irrepressible employer, serving Elsie with unswerving loyalty to the end.

ANIMAL PRINTS

A LA ELSIE

LEFT: Curtains of leopard-print cotton hung in a de Wolfe–decorated bathroom that incorporates both her trademark mirrored walls and black-and-white checkered floor. Painting by Julian LaTrobe.

CONTEMPORARY ECHOES OF ELSIE

OVERLEAF FROM LEFT: Painted walls repeat the fantasy animal print of the curtains in Geoffrey Beene's Long Island dining room.

Tawny leopard-skin velvet upholsters a pair of gilded Regency stools in a room with a bounty of burnished browns and sunny yellows.

SECOND OVERLEAF, CLOCKWISE FROM TOP LEFT: A mélange of animal prints—leopard on the chair, tiger-skin cushions, and ocelot-patterned rug—in a Paris apartment by interior designer Jean Louis Riccardi.

An oversized settee upholstered in leopard print and a rug with bold zebra stripings make strong counterpoints to the muted-colorings in a Manhattan living room designed by Roger Lusher.

Geoffrey Beene scatters dalmatian spots on a black-lacquer footrest.

ROYAL

As Lady Mendl, Elsie found her social horizons greatly expanded. Her decorating commissions brought her increasing wealth and celebrity. They included Condé Nast's fabulous Manhattan apartment, whose ballroom she elevated into a shimmering landscape with eighteenth-century Ch'ien Lung wallpaper, mirrors, and crystal chandeliers; and Commandant Paul-Louis Weiller's villa in Versailles, which she filled with fanciful murals and leopard-patterned carpets. Her glamorous and celebrated parties at the Villa Trianon were ultimately, however, to make her more famous than her interiors.

Invitations to Sunday lunch at the Villa Trianon were prized by those restless Americans and Europeans who traveled the world in the years between the wars. Hungry for entertainment and distraction, with money still plentiful, these social butterflies flocked to Elsie's parties. The attraction was definitely not the cuisine. Elsie was notoriously stingy about food, disliking large meals herself, disapproving of them for health reasons, and exploiting this principle as a splendid way to economize. What she provided—and improved upon with the help of her new husband—was a guest list of the most delightful eclecticism, ranging from fashion figures to diplomats, models to decorators, the flotsam and jetsam of noble houses to the occasional genuine royal.

Perhaps the perceptive observer might have noticed a slight change in the quality of entertainment at the Villa Trianon in those days. The artists, musicians, and writers whom Bessie Marbury had attracted in the early years— "superior minds," as Elsie herself described them—seemed to have given way to

ELSIE

more frivolous types, those anxious to advance in the social hierarchy, encouraged by the likes of Elsa Maxwell to insinuate themselves into the Mendl circle, where they would be sure to make socially useful connections.

It was said that Elsie, like Elsa, her close friend and cohostess at many of the parties, was quite possibly taking financial payoffs for offering these services. If so, it could perhaps be justified by the argument that Lady Mendl was, after all, still a professional woman. Her career as an interior decorator required her to expose prospective clients to art, antiques, and beautiful objects, which naturally enough were owned by people of taste and breeding. Besides that, she still had to earn a sizable amount of money to subsidize her extravagant way of life. Others were beginning to threaten her predominance in the field—Ruby Ross Wood (who had helped her write *The House in Good Taste*), Eleanor McMillen, and Sister Parish in the United States, and Syrie Maugham and Sybil Colefax in England, were all successful competitors. (Although when Syrie Maugham asked Elsie for ad-

vice, the prima donna of the profession is said to have retorted, "You're too late, my dear, much too late. The decorating field is already overcrowded.") Elsie's controversial buy-out of Anne Morgan's share in the Villa Trianon in 1928—which redounded greatly to Elsie's profit while creating lasting bitterness between the two old friends —only underscored Elsie's consistent and never-ending need for money. Her

early credo—"I loathe pover-
ty. I hate the sordid, the ugly,
and the cheap"—was one that
she never rescinded.

In yet one more search for
the perfect surroundings, Elsie
bought an apartment in 1931
that had formerly belonged to
Prince Roland de Bourbon on
the avenue d'Iéna. In it she de-
vised the one room above all
others that came to represent
her dream of perfection—the
bathroom salon. Elsie the icon-
oclast had done it again. She
took the room least charming,
least deserving of time and
money, least susceptible of
aesthetic interest, and turned
it into a triumph of elegance
and comfort, with fireplace,
mirrored friezes, a divan upholstered in bold zebra skin,

Elsie's salon de
bain *in her Paris
apartment on the
avenue d'Iéna.*

a tub surrounded
with all-mirrored

columns, taps in the shape of swans' heads, hooks in the form of dolphins, light fixtures gleaming with the luster of oyster shells and mother-of-pearl. "Moonshine and glamour, white orchids and rock crystal, silver tissue and white furs, reflected in many mirrors," Elsie once wrote in a full flight of lyricism. "That is my bathroom, believe it or not."

People did find it hard to believe. They poured into the Paris apartment to stare at this aquatic fantasy, and Elsie, perched on her zebra-skin sofa, received them proudly—in her *salon de bain*.

But even while Elsie lauded her live-in bathroom, the Depression was eating into her profits. Money problems were to dog her for the rest of her life, and stories of her financial finaglings became legendary. A case in point: She once lodged Ludwig Bemelmans (whom she called Stevie; he called her Mother) in a guestroom after a party, and in the morning the conversation went like this:

"Did you know who put you to bed last night?"
"I have no idea."
"Mother did."
"Thank you, Mother."
"And were you comfortable?"
"Yes, very."
"And warm?"
"Yes, warm."
"You know why you were warm and comfortable, Stevie?"
"No."
"Because Mother covered you with her best fur blanket."
"Thank you, Mother. God bless you."
"Stevie, do you like that blanket?"
"Yes, I like it very much."
"Well, Mother will give you that blanket, Stevie."
I said, "Thank you very much, Mother."
She paused. "Mother will give you that blanket for eight hundred dollars, Stevie."

ELSIE, CHIC AND SOIGNÉE IN HER SEVENTIES, PHOTOGRAPHED BY HER PROTÉGÉ CECIL BEATON.

Tightfisted in some areas, Elsie was generous to a fault in others. When Cecil Beaton, almost unknown in the late twenties, could not find a place to exhibit his photographs in New York, she not only offered her showroom but produced a handsome program to help sell them. Albert Hadley remembers Elsie's quirky generosity when he was a young decorator. He had picked up a portrait he felt sure was of her and asked a mutual friend, decorator James Amster, to show it to her to authenticate. Amster obliged, but Elsie seemed uncharacteristically vague about its validity. Soon after, Hadley was invited to one of Elsie's drink parties, and following the customary green-and-white fare (watercress sandwiches and the Lady Mendl cocktail, a concoction of Cointreau, gin, and grapefruit juice), he was introduced to his hostess. With a conspiratorial dig of her elbow, Elsie told him the sketch had been done from newspaper-file photographs and the artist had mistakenly put Anne Morgan's head on Elsie's body. "But let's say it's me," she cackled, "and that will make it much more valuable."

A shrewd financial move during Elsie's early days of fame as a fashion arbiter turned out to make considerably more money for her than selling fur blankets ever could. She invested in the Paris couture establishment of a Chicago-born designer named Main Bocher, whose clothes she then wore for the rest of her life. Mainbocher—the names were run together to form his stylish fashion signature —was her most successful investment, paying her handsome dividends each year ad infinitum. He was also a key player in the developing friendship between Elsie and one Mrs. Ernest Simpson.

Wallis Simpson and Elsie had been introduced in London by Johnnie Mc-Mullin, and they became friends. Elsie, by far the older woman, served as a sort of mentor for Wallis, whose social skills were not finely honed when she first

moved to England with her husband. When the American started her liaison with the Prince of Wales, Elsie stood staunchly by as social and fashion adviser to her newly elevated friend, and Mainbocher became a mainstay of Wallis's wardrobe. When the Prince of Wales ascended to the throne as Edward VIII in 1936, he sent a private plane to Paris to bring Elsie to Fort Belvedere, his bachelor resi-

dence, to discuss its redecoration. Later that year the notion of Elsie's taking on the sprucing up of Buckingham Palace was discussed, and Elsie must have held her breath at the thought of this ultimate pinnacle of recognition.

ABOVE: *ELSIE AND FAMOUS FRIENDS AT VERSAILLES, 1936.* BELOW: *ELSIE'S GUESTBOOK.*

She backed, on this occasion, the wrong horse. But credit should be given her for remaining loyal to the toppler of the English throne. Alice Keppel, longtime mistress of Edward VII, told Elsie that London society would never receive her again if she retained her connection to the wicked witch of Windsor. "At my age and in my position," Elsie replied with spirit, "the only door I am interested in is my

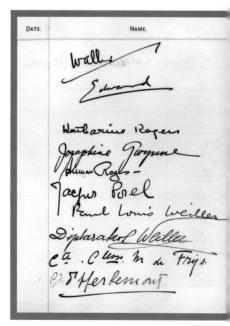

own—and I will open and close it to whom I choose." She opened it many times to the Windsors as they wandered in exile through France and after they settled in Paris. "For bringing together all kinds of people in a gay, airy, but flawless setting, I have never known anyone to equal Lady Mendl," the duchess, herself a student of Elsie's hospitality, was later to credit her friend. "She mixes people like a cocktail—and the result is sheer genius."

In 1937, Elsie's decorating business in New York declared bankruptcy. True to form, she had had the foresight to wriggle out a year earlier, and had already surrendered her interest. While the firm's demise was a sign of the times, it was also a revealing commentary on the latest turn Elsie's career had taken. The reason for her fame and fortune in the first place—and the original outlet for her talents —had ceased to exist. She was finally uprooted, separated from her past, freed from the moorings of her professional duties. For the rest of her life, she was to float in a kind of glittering limbo, encouraged by myriad admirers, invigorated by her varied surroundings, an icon of age and gender defied.

Elsie was seventy-two that year, ready to enter perhaps the most legendary

period of a long and flamboyant life. To foster the legend of her longevity, with typical iconoclasm she had come up with an ingenious notion. While most women of fashion tended to deduct as many years as were plausible from their true ages, Elsie added them, so that people, concluding she was already more than eighty, were doubly astonished at her evergreen performance.

For performance it was. By this time, she had almost entirely reinvented her appearance. In characteristic pioneering spirit, she confidently entrusted her body to various avant-garde experts—Erno Laszlo for skin, Antoine for hair, Gayelord Hauser for diet—all of whom in those days were considered somewhat radical. Face lifted, hair dyed blue, advanced techniques of makeup strategically applied, the diminutive, colorful, powdered and painted doll—dressed brilliantly by such dernier cri designers such as Chanel, Patou, and her protégé Mainbocher— seemed ultimately to have taken on an aura of immortality.

Elsie's body was pressed into ever-more strenuous service in the cause. She

ABOVE: *GOSSIP AND GAMESMANSHIP AT THE CELEBRATED VILLA TRIANON SUNDAY LUNCHES.*

had done exercises since she was a small child, and as a grown woman the regimen was unflinching. Eye exercises, leg and arm

When you hear that Lady Mendl standing up Now turns a handspring landing up On her toes, Anything goes!

Lyrics from Cole Porter's "Anything Goes"

stretches, and headstands were par for the course. At a fancy-dress ball in Paris, Princess Guy de Faucigny-Lucinge and Elsie made their entrance doing cartwheels. Though some guests questioned the propriety of a diplomat's wife performing acrobatics in a ballroom, Elsie was not to be deterred. "That I can turn handsprings shows what diet and exercise have done toward dissipating the fallacy that old age is a period of disintegration and senility."

Elsie's energy matched her dedication to fitness. She traveled abroad, as far as India. She was often accompanied by her adored poodles, each of which she buried with the epitaph "To the One I Love the Best." She wrote an autobiography, filled with her rules for physical and mental health, entitled *After All*. She continued to give decorating advice, for enormous fees, and to collect. She met more and more people, although not always with success. Diplomat and writer Valentine Lawford, a new recruit to the Mendl circle, was present when Elsie visited Gertrude Stein in her famous Paris salon with its dazzling collection of modern paintings. "There we met Salvador Dali, and of course Elsie said to him, 'Do you paint?' It was a scream." Lawford observed that "she and Gertrude are two very different examples of what the United States can produce. It was the only time I ever saw Elsie Mendl nonplussed by her surroundings and perceptibly uncomfortable."

Parties were the raison d'être of Elsie's life now, always bigger, madder, more exotic parties, with more and more elaborate themes—baby parties, murder parties, Apache parties, scavenger parties—all peopled by the glitterati of Europe and America, with Elsie at the helm, surrounded by Sir Charles, her bachelor boys, Elsa Maxwell, and her poodles, and written about with feverish excitement by the gossip columnists. The legend had been created and grew by the month. A sign of her fame was her appearance in popular

songs of the day. Cole Porter and Noël Coward among others wrote lyrics celebrating her, and Coward summed up the impact of the old trouper in his own impeccable fashion: "We talked about growing old gracefully/And Elsie, who's seventy-four/Said, 'A, it's a question of being sincere/And B, if you're supple you've nothing to fear,'/Then she swung upside down from a glass chandelier./I couldn't have liked it more!"

Who footed the bill for these extravaganzas? Elsie herself paid for the food—

those "simple dishes" she loved—and Sir Charles paid for the wine, which always flowed freely. She continued to squirrel money and commissions out of innocent victims, usually with nerve that would have earned the respect of a Mafia don. But in the background she nurtured a far more reliable patron, the industrialist Commandant Paul-Louis Weiller, whose generosity stretched to a very considerable extent the scale of Elsie's entertainments. He seems to have been totally and willingly in her thrall. "She was so delightful," he said later, "and her parties were so gay. One was really happy to help her pay."

So happy was Commandant Weiller with the pleasures of her company, that under his patronage Elsie was able to pull off the most fabulous party of her career, and the one above all others by which she was to be remembered. "My ambition has always been to have a private zoo," she once wrote. "The nearest I ever got to one were several little flying squirrels, some Siamese cats, and all sorts and varieties of highly bred dogs." In July 1938, Elsie fulfilled, albeit for only a day, her ambition, when she held her Circus Ball—which featured a real circus, with a tent, a ring, circus animals, bands, acrobats, jugglers, and, of course, a ringmaster—none other than Elsie herself. Fairylike in a white organdy gown by Mainbocher and an aquamarine and diamond tiara, she cracked a whip at eight trained circus ponies as they gracefully went through their paces for this starry elf and her legion of awestruck guests. Three orchestras and a Hawaiian guitarist strumming from a boat in the swimming pool rounded out the spectacle.

The circus tent was a vivid green-and-white-striped pavilion designed by

LEFT: *ELSIE'S CIRCUS BALL. CLOCKWISE FROM TOP LEFT: ACROBATS IN ACTION; ELSIE BETWEEN CHARLES AND DIPLOMAT SIR GEORGE CLERK; ELSIE THE RINGMASTER, PAINTED BY OLIVER MESSEL.*

Stéphane Boudin, the venerable French master decorator of the house of Jansen. It was a confection of Regency-style draperies, tufted white leather banquettes, and marble pillars. Elsie

so loved it that she left it standing as a permanent addition to the house, the glamorous setting for more parties at the Villa Trianon.

But for a second time in Elsie's life, a world war spoiled the fun. On September 3, 1939, France and England declared war on Germany—and once again chauffeurs and butlers disappeared overnight to enlist in the army, people panicked and fled, and the idea of the Germans entering Paris haunted everyone's sleep. This time, however, there was no Bessie to summon Elsie to the safety of the United States. This time, Elsie knew exactly where her place was, at home in France. The only adjustment she made was to close her avenue d'Iéna apartment and move to an equally grand suite at the Ritz Hotel, where the parties and salons continued, just as they continued on weekends at the Villa Trianon. It was only Elsie's husband who presented a problem, for Sir Charles was Jewish; and although, like a surprising number of British aristocrats, he had a sneaking admi-

ration for the Germans, he was well aware of the personal danger he faced by remaining in a country threatened with Nazi occupation.

The so-called phony war, which lasted into the late spring of 1940, lulled the Mendls, and much of France, into a false sense of security. The Nazis swiftly moved on Paris in June of that year, and once again Elsie and her entourage reluctantly packed up and fled south to the Spanish border. When they arrived, it was already closed and throngs of refugees were pressing at the gates in rage and desperation. One of the more bizarre moments in Elsie's career must surely have been the night she spent at the border, locked in her Rolls-Royce for safety's sake, ramrod-erect in the backseat with two poodles and stacks of Vuitton luggage, dressed to the nines in her jewels and her Mainbocher, while angry fellow refugees crowded around the Rolls, jeering and making fists at her through the windows.

BATH
SALONS

CONTEMPORARY ECHOES OF ELSIE

LEFT: The tub alcove in a bathroom by designer Robert D'Arid with the classic ambience and architectural detailing of an Empire salon.

OVERLEAF, CLOCKWISE FROM TOP LEFT: Vintage tub, side chairs, and a lacy wicker chaise for a read or a rest in a summer-seaside setting.

A Paris bathroom/study designed by Patrice Terrel has printed linen walls, a patterned carpet, and a table desk set between the windows.

Victoriana revisited—Michael La Rocca's parlor/bath with period feel and furniture incorporates both a whirlpool bath and modern lighting.

The dressing table moves to center stage, the bathtub turns into a cushion-covered banquette—and a bathroom becomes the dining room in this Parisian apartment by interior designer Christian Benais.

ELSIE

Elsie arrived safely by plane in New York in July of 1940, and set up temporary hotel housekeeping at the St. Regis. Manhattan welcomed her as an old friend, but a better place was waiting for Elsie, a place where many war refugees had migrated, a place with the money and glamour that by now had come to be requisite components of her life. What better prescription could there be for her than Hollywood? The house she bought with Sir Charles was reported to be the ugliest in Beverly Hills. Situated on Benedict Canyon Drive, the dark red adobe structure had huge rooms, with pretentious cathedral ceilings and arches; the garden consisted mostly of a swimming pool and a view of the back alley. Need-

GOES

less to say, Elsie soon changed all that. She painted the exterior white, hung the entrance with green-and-white-striped canvas curtains, used mostly dark green, white, and black for the interiors, and filled the rooms with mirrors, banquettes, and painted furniture. She got rid of the pool and planted the space with a huge olive tree surrounded by white begonias. She added a little mirrored garden pavilion and concealed the alley with mirrors. She called the house "After All," as she had titled her autobiography. By the end of her labors the place was, in a catchphrase of the forties, drop-dead dazzling—and if the Beverly Hills social arbiters had doubted the suitability of this nouvelle arriviste from Paris with her

HOLLYWOOD

fancy entourage of dogs, bachelors, and secretaries, Elsie's decorating brilliance, plus her own astonishing appearance, won all hearts. "It was a perfectly ordinary house," director George Cukor said, "but her personality made it lambent."

For four years Elsie lived and entertained in Southern California. If it was an exile, she hardly showed it. Her parties became as famous as those at the Villa Trianon, her guests numbering movie stars, writers, musicians, and a growing list of bright young men whose talents she encouraged and from whom her white gloves, turbans, headstands, mauve-tinted hair, strange jeweled accessories, and penchant for costumes evoked absolute adoration. She wrote a little book entitled *Elsie de Wolfe's Recipes for Successful Dining*, in which she spelled out her dinner-party rules (which mostly consisted of brevity in courses, and hot, hot, *hot* plates).

PRECEDING: *ELSIE AT HER DOORWAY IN BEVERLY HILLS.* LEFT: *THE INFORMAL LIVING ROOM, CURTAINED IN ELSIE'S SIGNATURE FERN PRINT.* ABOVE: *DUQUETTE CONSOLE BELOW FEATHER-FRAMED FLOWERS.* ABOVE RIGHT: *ELSIE AND TONY DUQUETTE.* RIGHT: *ELSIE IN THE GRAND SALON OF AFTER ALL.*

TOP: *ELSIE'S CALIFORNIA RUE DE RIVOLI—TWO VIEWS OF THE L-SHAPED VERANDA. ABOVE: THE DINING ROOM/BAR.*

She began insisting that people call her Mother, and dispensed wisdom and threw out orders in a way that delighted her adopted sons—among them Ludwig Bemelmans, who later celebrated her in his affectionate memoir, *To the One I Love the Best*, and James Amster, who became a distinguished New York decorator.

But the closest of Elsie's California aficionados was a young Los Angeles artist and designer, Tony Duquette, whose spectacular centerpiece at a dinner party had caught her critical eye. Within days, Elsie had Tony working for her —building intricate and elegant pieces of furniture, painting murals, creating objects of beauty that she bought enthusiastically and made other people buy. Abetted by Elsie's boosting and belief in his talent, his career soared internationally—and as president of the Elsie de Wolfe Foundation, he has remained the steadfast keeper of her flame through the years since her death.

During Elsie's wartime exile, only the restrictions of age dogged her otherwise irrepressible progress. Not that she accepted for a minute its limitations. She exercised. She ate sparingly, and carefully, on the orders of Gayelord Hauser. She had injections of a serum made from the cells of embryonic goats. She took weekly treatments of colonic irrigation. But because of arthritis she was reduced to traveling mostly in a wheelchair. She stayed in bed later, and retired earlier. She was often in great pain from her back. Yet there was never even a glimmer of self-pity. It was as though some inner fire were driving her. Clearly Elsie was husbanding her strength, waiting for the moment when she could return to its source—France, and her treasured Villa Trianon.

TROMPE L'OEIL

CONTEMPORARY ECHOES OF ELSIE

LEFT: Trompe l'oeil picture hangings and architectural decoration give linear form and style to a wall of diverse and varied-size paintings.

OVERLEAF FROM LEFT: Graphic artist André François's mural has a trompe l'oeil paved staircase leading to a faux second-story landing.

Nina Campbell uses bookcases, stonework, and paneled screens—all of them trompe l'oeil—to set off the staircase in her London duplex.

SECOND OVERLEAF FROM LEFT: Trompe l'oeil details of a dining room in Tuscany recall the grand gestures of traditional Italian decoration.

Ornamental trompe l'oeil—fluted columns, Empire moldings, swags, and still lifes—frame the corner bed in a country guestroom.

ELSIE'S

Elsie returned at last to postwar Paris in June 1946. The Villa Trianon had been inhabited by Nazi officers during the occupation, with horrific results—slashed upholstery, chandeliers ripped from ceilings, objets d'art stolen, porcelains and crystal broken, scrapbooks defaced, dirt and degradation everywhere. The prospect of restoring such devastation would have seemed impossible, surely, to anyone except Elsie de Wolfe, who—eighty-one years old, crippled by arthritis, financially strapped, emotionally exhausted—jumped into the fray without a moment's hesitation. The house, at least, was intact. Walls, windows, shrubberies, all were standing. Everything else could be repaired. To that end, Elsie wrote

LAST

letters, recruited workers, dispensed largesse, and enlisted everybody she knew who could be useful in bringing the house back to its former glory. The task was daunting. Postwar conditions were hard, materials in short supply, and priorities for craftsmen and seamstresses did not include the restoration of an elderly American's villa. But indomitable Elsie succeeded; the old friends were soon eagerly making their threadbare way back to the prewar scene of so much fondly remembered merriment and flamboyance. They could not help noticing how much their hostess had changed. "There she was in a small wheelchair by the pool," recalled Jean-Louis Faucigny-Lucinge, "looking terribly pathetic . . . in great pain . . .

STAND

surrounded by her dogs, very made-up, still, and determined not to give in."

Elsie fought death like the gladiator she was. Sick and suffering, she would suddenly revive for some revelry. "Oh, a party!" she'd cry. "Well, I must get up." Ludwig Bemelmans describes Elsie before one of her last parties:

> The candles were being lit, the room was ready, and Mother came down the stairs as usual. She wore one of her Mainbocher uniforms, and as always at the beginning of the cocktail hour, she staggered a bit with age until she found somebody's arm. But then, after a while, the motor started; she always straightened up, kicked herself free, steadied herself, and was on her own. She pulled at her skirt so that it sat right; she pulled at it on both sides, like a little girl about to sit down in a new party dress—and she started her circle.

Elsie de Wolfe died on July 12, 1950, at eighty-five—though many people believed her wicked ruse about her age and thought her well over ninety. To the last she protested: *"Je ne veux pas mourir, je ne veux pas m'en aller."*

At Elsie's request, there was no funeral. Her will was typically idiosyncratic. (She fell asleep during its preparation and woke up to hear the lawyer reading out her list of bequests. "And what do I get?" she demanded. "You get nothing, Lady Mendl," the lawyer said with admirable restraint. "Ha!" she bellowed. "Why don't I get anything?" "Because you are dead," replied the lawyer.) She bequeathed the bulk of her small fortune to the stalwart Hilda West. Sir Charles was left a modest yearly income. The rest went to the foundation Elsie established to provide scholarships for young designers and to carry on her charities.

As for the disposition of Elsie's true love, the Villa Trianon, it turned out that in perhaps her most startling coup of all, she had made a secret pact with her old friend and neighbor Paul-Louis Weiller. Elsie had sold him the house and all

PRECEDING: *DETAILS FROM ELSIE'S BEDROOM DOOR IN THE VILLA TRIANON.* its contents in 1931, with the proviso that she could continue living in it until her death. In 1948 she sold him her pearls as well, at a hugely inflated price, under the condition that she could wear them as long as she lived. Possession was Elsie's, the pleasure of patronage Weiller's—a happy arrangement on both sides.

In retrospect, the pearls and the haute couture were spectacular, the parties and high jinx fun—but ephemeral. The true memorial to Elsie de Wolfe is her lasting influence on the decorating profession both in America and in Europe. It is her pioneering spirit, her innovative ideas, and her unerring eye that have made an indelible mark upon the decorative arts of the twentieth century and have earned her a modest place in the social history of our time.

As usual, clear-eyed Elsie knew herself best: "I can't paint, I can't write, I can't sing. But I can decorate and run a house, and light it, and heat it, and have it like a living thing and so right that it will be the envy of the world, the standard of perfect hospitality."

ACKNOWLEDGMENTS This book began in 1986 with an illustrated lecture on Elsie de Wolfe's pioneering role in modern interior decoration given by Nina Campbell at London's Victoria and Albert Museum. Through the years since then, a great many people have made generous contributions to the mix of this potpourri portrait in which we have tried to capture the essence of Elsie. To all of them, the authors and the editor are more than grateful.

At Clarkson Potter: Carol Southern, Howard Klein, Jane Treuhaft, Joan Denman, Mark McCauslin, Ed Otto, Laurie Stark, Eliza Scott, Bill Nave, Bernadine Edwards, Barbara Marks, Phyllis Fleiss, Allan Eady, Lisa Plattner, Lisa Keim, and Joan De Mayo.

At Random House: Robert Bernstein, Howard Kaminsky, Anne Yarowsky, Carol Schneider, Jane Opper, Christy Archibald, Robert Scudellari, Iris Weinstein, Edward McGill, and the late Dennis Dwyer.

At Condé Nast: Dania Martinez Davey, Dierdre Dolan, Nancy Novogrod, Diana Edkin, Cynthia Cathcart, Fred Keith, and Leo Lerman.

In New York: Stanley Barrows, Keith Irvine, Albert Hadley, Dasha Epstein, Susan McCone, Mario Buatta, Barry Friedman, Mark Hampton, Anthony Victoria, Daniel Pearl, Paul Manno, George Trescher, Henry Hyde, Ellen Horan, Rose Ann Leary, Barbara Kantor, Helen Skor, Robert Montgomery, Fayal Green, Robin Roberts, Susan Freedman, John Knott, Brigitta Williamson, Richard Johan, John Miller, Betty Sheets, the late James Amster, and Alexandra Danilova.

In London: Stephen Calloway, Hugo Vickers, Bettina and Henry McNulty, Nancy Lancaster, Tim Chadwick, Michael Alcock, Piers Burnett, Meredith Etherington-Smith, Gillon Aitken, Fleur Ogilvie, Isabelle Greenwood, Keith Lamborne, Elizabeth Glendevon, and John McCullough.

In Paris: Commandant Paul-Louis Weiller, Nenette Hazak, Samantha Thomas, Burnet Pavitt, and André Ostier.

In California: Tony Duquette, Hutton Wilkinson, Gep Durenberger, Maurice Gibson, and Stanford Stevenson.

Jane Treuhaft's infallible eye, Mark McCauslin's impeccable pencil, and Joan Denman's production legerdemain have played major roles in the way this book looks and reads. And it's doubtful that this account of Elsie would have happened without Albert Hadley's time, trouble, and generosity from the very beginning. They have our heartfelt gratitude and our special thanks.

Copywork/transparencies: Fred Valentine and Ken Kothé of Color Media, Jacques Backmann, Pamela Risio of Applied Graphics Technologies, and Tom Sauerwein.

ARCHIVAL PHOTOGRAPHS   Elsie de Wolfe was one of the first international celebrities. She came on the New York scene as a young amateur actress in the 1880s and never left center stage until her death in 1950. Her vivid personality, her free-wheeling lifestyle, and her very real accomplishments made her irresistible to the popular press and the chroniclers of fashion and society. The archival photographs in this book that document Elsie's life and career from childhood through her Hollywood heyday come mainly from the splendid public and private collections of record that are among the treasures of New York City. The rest have been gleaned from the memorabilia of de Wolfe devotees here and abroad.

82
Elsie's set for a 1915 musical comedy. *Billy Rose Theatre Collection, New York Public Library*

83
Elsie in 1915 and in 1919. *Vogue**

90
Elsie and Charles on the Lido. *Topham*

92–93
Bessie Marbury's Sutton Place house. *New York Public Library*
The Sutton Place drawing room. Anne Morgan's Sutton Place morning room. *Vogue**

94–95
Charles and Elsie on their honeymoon. *Vogue**
Charles at ease.
Elsie and Charles.
An alfresco lunch party at Versailles. *Collection of Burnet Pavitt*

106–107
Condé Nast apartment. *Vogue**

113–114
Elsie and friends at Versailles.
Villa Trianon alfresco lunch. *Collection of Burnet Pavitt*

116
Elsie standing on her head. *After All*, Elsie de Wolfe

118
Top left and right: Elsie's Circus Ball. *Vogue**

128, 132
After All, Elsie's house in Beverly Hills. *Vogue**

* *Courtesy Vogue. Copyright © 1914, 1915, 1919, 1921, 1926, 1928, 1938, 1943, 1949, 1952, 1953, 1954, 1956, 1957, 1966, 1971 by The Condé Nast Publications, Inc.*

BIBLIOGRAPHY That her voice was as inimitable as her eye was surely no hindrance to Elsie's enduring fame. She had a whim of iron, her opinions were forged in steel—and what she had to say and the way she said it influenced, amused, and sometimes confounded her listeners and readers alike. In our account of Elsie—especially when it comes to her decorating principles and practices—we have for the most part allowed her to speak for herself, drawing from her magazine articles, her landmark book on decoration, *The House in Good Taste*, and her autobiography, *After All*. We are indebted to Jane Smith, whose definitive biography of Elsie so brilliantly untangled the web of fact and fiction woven by the wily Ms. de Wolfe, and to the late Ludwig Bemelmans, whose affectionate memoir of Elsie is a love letter she would have cherished.

Bemelmans, Ludwig. *To the One I Love Best*. New York: Viking, 1955.

de Wolfe, Elsie. *After All*. New York: Harper & Brothers, 1935.

———. "Châteaux in Touraine." *Cosmopolitan*, February 1891.

———. *Elsie de Wolfe's Recipes for Successful Dining*. New York: D. Appleton–Century Co., 1934.

———. *The House in Good Taste*. New York: The Century Co., 1915.

———. "A Romance of Old Shoes." *Cosmopolitan*, April 1892.

———. "Stray Leaves from My Book of Life." *Metropolitan* XIV (1901).

Smith, Jane S. *Elsie de Wolfe*. New York: Atheneum, 1982.

FABRICS   Chintz was the medium that heralded Elsie's message of a new kind of American interior decoration. Always her mainstay, she used it in every permutation—flowered, striped, and in prints from chinoiserie to toile de Jouy. As a backbone of this book, we have reproduced examples from the extraordinary array of chintzes currently available through international fabric houses—an homage to Elsie's insistence that "chintz, when properly used, is the most decorative and satisfactory of all fabrics." Another Elsie signature, fabrics with exotic animal patterns like zebra and jaguar, appeared again and again in de Wolfe rooms over the decades. The reader will surely observe that leopard-print velvet was Elsie's clear favorite.

ECHOES OF ELSIE There is no more positive proof of Elsie de Wolfe's long-lasting legacy to the world of decorating than the echoes of her ideas and innovations in the work of today's design talents. This book presents a spectrum of contemporary rooms that incorporate the evergreen de Wolfe dictums—vividly recorded by the skillful photographers credited here.

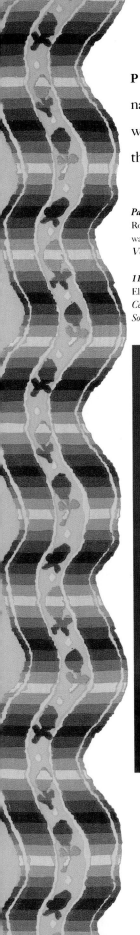

P O R T R A I T S   Painters and photographers from Boldini to Beaton were fascinated by Elsie—perhaps because while her spirit and character were steadfast, her image was ever-evolving, always a reflection of the times. The portraits in this book trace both the constancy and the chameleon changes that were quintessential Elsie.

Page 104
Royal Elsie in a 1935 Cecil Beaton
watercolor.
*Vogue**

111
Elsie in the 1930s, by Cecil Beaton.
*Cecil Beaton Archive, courtesy of
Sotheby's London*

144
Watercolor of Elsie in 1930 by
Cecil Beaton.
Courtesy of Bettina and Henry McNulty

146
Elsie in 1927, photographed by
Nickolas Muray.
*Vogue**

150
Left: Elsie in 1924, photographed by
Edward Steichen.
Right: Elsie in 1928, photographed by
George Hoyningen-Heuné.
*Vogue**

151
Elsie in 1930, painted by Bernard Boutet
de Monvel.
*Courtesy of the Barry Friedman Gallery of
New York, Ltd.*

*Courtesy Vogue. Copyright © 1924,
1927, 1928, 1935, 1952, 1955,
1956, 1963 by The Condé Nast
Publications, Inc.*

ELSIE DE WOLFE FOUNDATION Far from a fusty institution, the Elsie de Wolfe Foundation conducts an ongoing celebration of its formidable progenitor. With palpable pride and affection, the directors have kept Elsie's memory alive, through the years supporting projects that surely would have been close to her heart. In the case of this book, the foundation's president, Tony Duquette, and its ubiquitous liaison, Hutton Wilkinson, have been endlessly generous in providing information, inspiration, and invaluable pictures. We are particularly grateful to them for leading us to Julian LaTrobe, whose remarkable oil renderings of major de Wolfe rooms are a chief ornament to our pages.

PAUL-LOUIS WEILLER Our final obeisance goes to Commandant Paul-Louis Weiller, whose unswerving friendship and patronage helped make many of Elsie's dreams come true. Aside from being grateful for his personal reminiscences and snapshots, we have Commandant Weiller to thank for the rare color photographs of the Villa Trianon in this book. It was he who for thirty years kept Elsie's pristine rooms just as she had left them in 1950—until contemporary photography could capture the palette, the proportions, and the unique personality of her magnum opus.

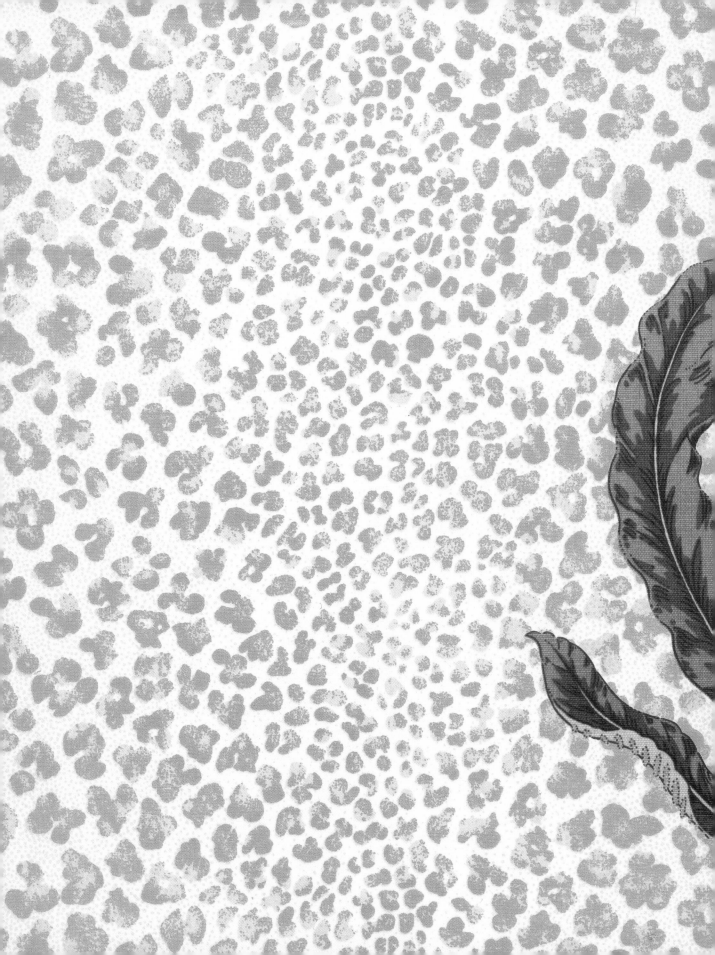